OF MICE AND MEN

A Kinship of Powerlessness

TWAYNE'S MASTERWORK STUDIES

Robert Lecker, General Editor

OF MICE AND MEN

A Kinship of Powerlessness

Charlotte Cook Hadella

TWAYNE PUBLISHERS
An Imprint of Simon & Schuster Macmillan
New York

Prentice Hall International
London Mexico City New Delhi Singapore Sydney Toronto

Twayne's Masterwork Studies No. 147

Of Mice and Men: A Kinship of Powerlessness
Charlotte Cook Hadella

Copyright © 1995 by Twayne Publishers

Twayne Publishers
An Imprint of Simon & Schuster Macmillan
1633 Broadway
New York, NY 10019

Library of Congress Cataloging-in-Publication Data

Hadella, Charlotte.
    Of mice and men : a kinship of powerlessness / Charlotte Hadella.
        p.   cm.—(Twayne's masterwork studies; no. 147)
    Includes bibliographical references and index.
    ISBN 0-8057-8589-2 (alk. paper)—ISBN 0-8057-8590-6 (pbk. : alk. paper)
    1. Steinbeck, John, 1902–1968. Of mice and men. 2. Power (Social sciences) in literature. I. Title. II. Series.
PS3537.T3234O27 1995
813'.52—dc20   94-49322
                                                                                CIP

10 9 8 7 6 5 4 3 2
10 9 8 7 6 5 4 3 2   (pbk.)

Printed in the United States of America.

For Paul and Lucia

Contents

Acknowledgments   ix

Chronology: John Steinbeck's Life and Works   xi

LITERARY AND HISTORICAL CONTEXT

    1. Historical Context   3

    2. The Importance of the Work   8

    3. Critical Reception   17

A READING

    4. An Experiment in Form   27

    5. Layers of Complexities: Reality, Symbol, and Myth   33

    6. Stage and Screen   64

Notes and References   83

Selected Bibliography   87

Index   95

Acknowledgments

Versions of parts of this manuscript appeared in *John Steinbeck: The Years of Greatness, 1936–1939,* edited by Tetsumaro Hayashi (Tuscaloosa: University of Alabama Press, 1993), 64–74; in *The Steinbeck Question: New Essays in Criticism,* edited by Donald R. Noble (Troy, N.Y.: Whitston Publishing Company, 1993), 51–70; and in *A New Study Guide to Steinbeck's Major Works, with Critical Explications,* edited by Tetsumaro Hayashi (Metuchen, N.J.: Scarecrow Press, 1993), 139–63.

I wish to thank Louis Owens for his Steinbeck seminar at the University of New Mexico, for encouraging my scholarship from its earliest beginnings, and for introducing me to Tetsumaro Hayashi and the International John Steinbeck Society. I also owe many thanks to Tetsumaro Hayashi for the attention he has given my work and for his tireless efforts over the years on behalf of Steinbeck scholarship on an international front. Thanks, too, to Susan Shillinglaw and the Steinbeck Research Institute for encouragement and photographs. I am indebted to the School of Arts and Letters at Southern Oregon State College for the research release time that gave me the opportunity to begin this work.

John Steinbeck

Courtesy of the Steinbeck Research Center, San Jose State University, San Jose, Calif.

Chronology: John Steinbeck's Life and Works

1902   John Steinbeck born 27 February in Salinas, California, to
            John Steinbeck and Olive Hamilton Steinbeck, youngest of
            four children and only son.

1919   Graduates from Salinas High School in the spring and enrolls
            at Stanford University in the fall.

1920   During a hiatus from Stanford, works on a Spreckels ranch
            near Salinas and observes firsthand the lives of bindle stiffs and
            ranch bosses, characters who would later become fictionalized
            in *Of Mice and Men*.

1922   Works nights at the Spreckels sugar refinery with Mexican
            nationals and picks up stories and characters that would
            appear in *Tortilla Flat*.

1923   Along with his sister Mary, enrolls for a summer quarter at
            Hopkins Marine Station in Pacific Grove, California, the
            beginning of his lifelong fascination with marine biology.

1924   Several of Steinbeck's stories appear in the Stanford *Spectator*,
            including "Fingers of Cloud" (which describes a young
            woman's encounter with a group of farmworkers, an early
            working of the sexual dynamics that would be played out more
            fully in *Of Mice and Men*).

1925   Drops out of Stanford permanently and takes a summer job as
            handyman at a Fallen Leaf Lake resort near Lake Tahoe. In
            November, boards a freighter from Los Angeles to New York,
            where he intends to make his name as a writer. Gets the idea
            for *Cup of Gold*, his first novel, while passing through the
            Panama Canal. Works briefly for the newspaper *American*, but
            has no success publishing his fiction in New York. Works vari-
            ous odd jobs, but is unable to make a living.

1926	Returns to Fallen Leaf Lake for a job as winter caretaker. Begins *Cup of Gold,* meets Carol Henning, and convinces her to type his manuscript.
1929	After many revisions, *Cup of Gold* is published and mistakenly promoted as a book for adolescents. The novel does not sell.
1930	Meets Ed Ricketts, marries Carol Henning, and moves to Pacific Grove. Fails to find a publisher for *To a God Unknown;* begins writing stories for *Pastures of Heaven.* Meets Joseph Campbell, Jungian and mythologist.
1932	*Pastures of Heaven* is published but does not sell well. Steinbeck revises *To a God Unknown* and moves for a short time to Los Angeles.
1933	*To a God Unknown* is published, but sales are dismal. The Steinbecks return to Pacific Grove. Sitting daily at the bedside of his dying mother, Steinbeck writes stories that will make up *The Red Pony,* the first two parts of which appear in *North American Review.*
1934	"The Murder" appears in *O. Henry Prize Stores.* Mother dies.
1935	*Tortilla Flat* is published; it sells well and wins the Commonwealth Club of California Gold Medal. His financial woes at an end, Steinbeck begins researching the farm labor novel *In Dubious Battle.* Travels in Mexico with Carol from September to December; returns to Pacific Grove via New York, where he signs film contract for *Tortilla Flat* just before Christmas.
1936	*In Dubious Battle* is published; though fairly well received, it raises controversy about Steinbeck's supposed Marxism. Works on *Of Mice and Men.* Father dies. Moves to Los Gatos and writes eight articles for the *San Francisco News.*
1937	*Of Mice and Men* is published and becomes a best-seller. The Theatre Union in San Francisco performs *Of Mice and Men* directly from the novel, 21 May–31 July. Meanwhile, Steinbeck writes the stage version, which is produced by George Kaufman on Broadway in November and wins the New York Drama Critics' Circle Award. The Steinbecks travel in Europe.
1938	Finishes writing "L'Affaire Lettuceberg," the earliest version of *The Grapes of Wrath;* burns the draft and begins again. Completes new draft in December; Carol names it *The Grapes of Wrath. The Long Valley* and *Their Blood Is Strong* are published.

Chronology

1939   *The Grapes of Wrath* is published and is a best-seller. Though denounced in Congress for his radical novel, Steinbeck is elected to the National Institute of Arts and Letters. *Of Mice and Men* is filmed.

1940   *The Grapes of Wrath* wins the Pulitzer Prize. Steinbeck makes collecting trip (for samples of marine life) to Gulf of California with Ed Ricketts. Works on filming *The Forgotten Village* in Mexico; *The Grapes of Wrath* is filmed.

1941   *Sea of Cortez: A Leisurely Journey of Travel and Research,* from Steinbeck's and Ricketts's journals during the Gulf of California trip, is published. *The Forgotten Village* is published in book form.

1942   *Bombs Away,* propaganda piece, written and published for the Army Air Corps. *The Moon Is Down,* Steinbeck's second play-novella, is published and becomes immensely popular in Northern Europe. Divorced from Carol Henning.

1943   Marries Gwyndolen Conger, 29 March, in New Orleans. Leaves Gwyn in New York and sails for England and North Africa as a war correspondent for the New York *Herald Tribune.* Returns from war after several months and establishes residency in New York. Works on scripts for the Hitchcock movie *Lifeboat* and, with Jack Wagner, the propaganda film *A Medal for Benny.*

1944   First son, Thom, born 2 August. *Lifeboat* is released; Steinbeck demands that his name be removed from the list of credits because he disapproves of what he perceives to be racism in the film.

1945   *Cannery Row* and *The Red Pony* published. *The Pearl* appears in *Woman's Home Companion* as "The Pearl of the World."

1946   Second son, John IV, born 12 June.

1947   *The Pearl* published as a novel. *The Wayward Bus* is published. Travels to Russia with photographer Robert Capa.

1948   *A Russian Journal* (Steinbeck's writing, Capa's photos) is published. Steinbeck and Gwyn Conger are divorced. Steinbeck's closest friend, Ed Ricketts, dies. The author is selected to the American Academy of Arts and Letters.

1949   Film version of *The Red Pony* released. Steinbeck works on script for Darryl F. Zannuck movie *Viva Zapata!*

1950   *Viva Zapata!* released. *Burning Bright,* another experimental play-novella, published. Steinbeck marries Elaine Scott.

1951   *The Log from the Sea of Cortez,* with Steinbeck's preface "About Ed Ricketts," is published.

1952   *East of Eden* is published. On assignment for *Colliers,* Steinbeck and Elaine travel to Europe.

1954   *Sweet Thursday* is published. The Steinbecks spend nine months in Europe, where Steinbeck writes for *Figaro* in Paris and begins *The Short Reign of Pippin IV,* a novella set in Paris.

1955   *Pipe Dream,* the musical comedy version of *Sweet Thursday,* is produced in New York, adapted by Richard Rogers and Oscar Hammerstein. The play is a failure. Steinbeck buys a house in Sag Harbor, Long Island.

1957   *The Short Reign of Pippin IV: A Fabrication* is published. Travels to Europe and researches Malory in preparation for a "translation" of *Morte d'Arthur.*

1958   *Once There Was a War,* a collection of dispatches written during World War II, is published. Steinbeck returns to England for Malory research.

1959   Spends the year in England working on his version of *Morte d'Arthur.*

1960   Returns to the United States and takes cross-country trip that will lead to his writing *Travels with Charley.*

1961   *The Winter of Our Discontent,* Steinbeck's last novel, is published. Travels to Europe with Elaine and both sons.

1962   The Steinbecks return to the United States. *Travels with Charley in Search of America* is published. Steinbeck is awarded the Nobel Prize for Literature.

1963   Travels to Eastern Europe with playwright Edward Albee.

1964   President Lyndon Johnson awards Steinbeck the Presidential Medal of Freedom. Pascal Covici, lifelong friend and editor, dies. Steinbeck travels to Ireland for Christmas.

1965   Travels to Europe and London. Sister Mary Dekker dies. Spends Christmas in Ireland.

1966   Travels to Israel on assignment for *Newsday. America and Americans* is published. Travels to Southeast Asia for *Newsday* as war in Vietnam intensifies.

1968   Suffers heart attack at Sag Harbor in May, a second attack in New York in July. Dies 20 December in New York City.

1969   The *East of Eden* letters, written to Covici, are published as *Journal of a Novel.*

1975   *The Acts of King Arthur and His Noble Knights,* unfinished draft of Steinbeck's version of *Morte d'Arthur,* is published.

LITERARY AND
HISTORICAL CONTEXT

1

Historical Context

The Great Depression of the 1930s, while it intensified the psychological need for believing in the American dream, also created an economic climate in which the achievement of that dream seemed more remote than ever for many segments of the American population. As the gap widened between the "haves" and the "have nots," American social economic thinking of the 1930s often pitted corporate society against communist labor organizers who sought to educate workers as to the value of their labor. Warren French, in *The Social Novel at the End of an Era*, refers to the social polarization of the late 1930s as an "era of what seemed the suicide of individualism."[1] Also prevalent at this time, however, was what could be described as a third voice: a back-to-the-farm movement that idealized the mystical bond between the human race and the soil, a philosophical stance that promoted self-realization and independence as direct by-products of living close to the land, as in small-scale family farming. French discusses a number of publications, from periodical articles to books with titles such as *Five Acres and Independence, Rural Roads to Security,* and *A Place in the Country,* which contributed to the public conversation in the 1930s about how to beat the Depression (French 1966, 61–82). It is this alternative to monopoly capitalism on the one hand and communism on the other that John Steinbeck cultivated as the central illusion of the main characters in *Of Mice and Men* (1937), the play-novelette that appears in Steinbeck's canon between two of his most powerful agrarian conflict novels, *In Dubious Battle* (1936) and *The Grapes of Wrath* (1939).

Born in Salinas, California, just after the turn of the century, Steinbeck grew up in the midst of the struggle for fair labor practices particular to large-scale agriculture that depended on a migrant labor force for economic viability. In the late nineteenth century, agriculture had emerged as California's leading industry—an industry plagued from the beginning by labor problems. As commercial growers took over more and more territory, squeezing out family farmers, the demand for cheap, seasonal labor intensified, and community structures deteriorated. Though traditional agrarianists argued for a return to small farms as a solution to farm labor difficulties and civic instability, the rise of commercial farming and the economic success of agribusiness sufficiently silenced the idealistic notion of a good society shared by all citizens of a democracy.[2]

Steinbeck carefully observed farm labor difficulties, usually from the point of view of the laborer. As a young college student dropping in and out of classes at Stanford University in the early 1920s, Steinbeck worked on the Spreckels Sugar Ranches near Salinas. This experience brought the budding writer into direct contact with migrant workers, many of whom were foreign nationals: Japanese, Filipino, and Mexican. In fact, Mexicans had become the mainstay of the agricultural labor force in California by the mid-1920s as growers took advantage of the liberalized federal immigration policy toward Mexico and as the flow of illegal immigration from Mexico steadily increased (Daniel, 67). Added to this mix were a number of Americans of Anglo-Saxon stock whose ancestors had migrated westward from the eastern or midwestern regions of the United States in the nineteenth century; though they originally sought their fortunes in gold and land, many eventually hired on as wage earners for the lucky entrepreneurs who had beaten them to the American dream.

4

His experience with the multinational labor force of California agribusiness exposed Steinbeck to a kaleidoscope of dialects, customs, and characters, all of which became material for his fiction. One of his earliest published stories, "Fingers of Cloud" (1924), takes place in the bunkhouse of a Filipino work gang. *Tortilla Flat* (1935), his first commercial success, details the lives of the *paisanos,* people of Spanish-Mexican descent who lived in the hills above Monterey. Juan Chicoy, a Mexican Indian, is the central character in *The Wayward Bus* (1947). Given the multiracial configuration of the California labor force in the early decades of the twentieth century, we may conclude that in *Of Mice and Men*, where the laborers are white Americans, Steinbeck did not intend to draw an accurate sociohistorical picture. Still, the subsistence-level economy, the tensions between workers and owners, and the social marginality of the migrant workers in the novella ring true to the historical details of the actual setting.

Furthermore, by focusing in *Of Mice and Men* on the dream of owning land, Steinbeck was appealing to a basic desire of average citizens as well as the dispossessed masses, regardless of their race or homeland. Steinbeck biographer Jackson Benson notes that while Steinbeck and his wife Carol were living in Mexico City for several months in 1935, the author was deeply moved by the struggles of the landless poor.[3] This experience, combined with his firsthand observations of the miserable lives of migrant laborers, began to take shape in Steinbeck's imagination as an experimental novel, written like a play, that would dramatize the struggles of working people who were striving to become independent landowners.

The Great Depression, of course, intensified labor tensions in the farming industry in California. In the early 1930s, agricultural wages dropped to all-time lows and workers found it difficult to provide food, shelter, and clothing for themselves and their dependents (Benson, 293). Even before the Communist party appeared on the scene, California workers had begun to strike against the unfair practices of growers. In 1932, the Cannery and Agricultural Workers' Industrial Union was organized by the Communist party, and the frequency and intensity of farm labor strikes in the valley increased. It was difficult for anyone living in California in the early 1930s not to be acutely aware of farm labor issues: strikes erupted in the Imperial Valley, the San Joaquin Valley, Watsonville, Salinas, and the Santa Clara Valley. Young people who were helping to organize the strikes and ministering to the needs of migrant families were dropping by the Steinbecks' cottage in Pacific Grove on a regular basis. Also during this period, Steinbeck became interested in writing a biographical piece about the labor organizers; through a friend and organizer, Francis Whitaker, Steinbeck was able to meet people associated with leftist activities and sympathetic to the plight of the workers (Benson, 293–97). As Louis Owens points out,

> [t]hough he never wrote the biographical story he had in mind, this meeting began a process of education for Steinbeck that would culminate in the short stories entitled "The Vigilante" and "The Raid," as well as Steinbeck's greatest novels, *In Dubious Battle, Of Mice and Men,* and *The Grapes of Wrath.* While, contrary to widespread opinion, Steinbeck was never sympathetic to communism, the author's sympathies would from this time forward lie more and more with the oppressed migrant laborer, and his lifelong loathing of middle-class materialism would evolve into a powerful resentment of corporate agriculture in California.[4]

Furthermore, the characters of those great works of the 1930s were knocking on Steinbeck's door, so to speak, without even being invited. In writing *In Dubious Battle,* Steinbeck took note of the events unfolding before him to dramatize what he considered to be "the symbol of man's eternal, bitter warfare with himself" (Benson, 304). He was interested in depicting the dynamics of a group-man, a phalanx theory that would explain mob psychology and blind commitment to a cause in scientific terms. Thus the work took on a documentary tone.

Having succeeded in portraying a large-scale battle between workers and growers in *In Dubious Battle,* Steinbeck turned his attention to the more private struggle of two migrant workers longing to escape from a cycle of oppression by buying a small farm of their own. By 1936, the year Steinbeck was writing *Of Mice and Men,* the technological revolution in agribusiness was threatening what little job security itinerant workers had. Anne Loftis reports that mechanical combines enabling 5 men to do the work of 350 men were responsible for half the nation's grain harvest in 1938.[5] Cletus E. Daniel, in *Bitter Harvest: A History of California Farmworkers, 1870–1941,* writes that "[b]y the twentieth century, employment in California's large-scale agriculture had come to mean irregular work, constant movement, low wages, squalid working and living conditions, social isolation, emotional deprivation, and individual powerlessness so profound as to make occupational advancement a virtual impossibility." He goes on to stress that "whatever the differences of race, national origin, language, and psychology that existed among farmworkers in California from 1870 to 1930, working for wages in industrialized agriculture normally conferred membership in an unhappy fraternity whose cohering force was a kinship of powerlessness" (Daniel, 64).

In *Of Mice and Men,* Steinbeck features just such an "unhappy fraternity": barley buckers, a bunkhouse hand, a mule skinner, a stable buck, and a lonely woman. These characters are thrust into conflict with the ranch owner, his son, and a social structure that views them more as expendable commodities than as worthwhile human beings. They are challenged to discover and to maintain their humanity in the face of overwhelmingly dehumanizing forces. In this sense, their story is not just an American drama that takes place in a particular region of the country at a particular time in history; it is a human drama for all places and all times.

2

The Importance of the Work

By the time he was composing *Of Mice and Men,* Steinbeck had survived the poverty of his literary apprenticeship and achieved commercial success with *Tortilla Flat.* Along with that success, however, came an unwelcome notoriety for the actual residents of Tortilla Flat and public intrusion into Steinbeck's private life, which made him uncomfortable. *In Dubious Battle* also sold well and received respectable critical assessments, though Steinbeck resented readers who viewed the novella as a documentary tract rather than a work of fiction. In fact, producing a piece of propaganda was the furthest thing from Steinbeck's mind as he wrote *In Dubious Battle;* his intent was to present both sides of the labor issue in as unbiased a perspective as his artistic powers would allow.

As Sylvia Cook explains quite clearly in "Steinbeck, the People, and the Party," in the novels of the 1930s Steinbeck was searching for literary symbols to express the biological themes of interest to him: group man (groups of human beings behaving as a single organism, with individual members behaving as cells within the organism), non-teleological thinking (concern with things as they exist rather than how or why they came to be), and "a holistic sense of unity and interdependency of all life forms and their environments."[1] He found these symbols in his immediate experience as a resident of California's central valley; coincidentally, the plight of the migrant worker in California took on national political significance during the decade.

That *In Dubious Battle* inspired criticism from both Communists and anti-Communists indicates that Steinbeck achieved his goal of nonpartisanship; yet being the center of an ideological feud did not agree with him. In an outburst of frustration, he wrote to Mavis McIntosh, his agent:

> [T]he damned people of both sides . . . postulate either an ideal communist or a thoroughly damnable communist and neither side is willing to suspect that the communist is a human, subject to the weaknesses and to the greatnesses of humans. I am not angry in the least. But the blank wall of stupid refusal even to look at the thing without colored glasses of some kind gives me a feeling of overwhelming weariness and a desire to run away and let them tear their stupid selves to pieces.[2]

Rather than run away from his critics, however, Steinbeck overcame his weariness by concentrating on ideas for new pieces of writing; among them was the early manuscript of *Of Mice and Men*.

At this stage in his career, and apparently throughout his life, Steinbeck was more concerned with his craft than with the responses of readers. An avid reader himself, Steinbeck was well aware of the modernist tradition that dominated the first two decades of twentieth-century literature, characterized by the use of myth and formal experimentation. Having come to the realization that he could never fully anticipate how his readership would react to his work, Steinbeck wrote to please himself. His artistic aims paralleled the modernist impulse to question prevailing assumptions about art, ethics, and society.[3] With *Of Mice and Men*, as with *In Dubious Battle* and other works, it appears that Steinbeck did not wish to assume a shared reality with his readers; rather, he wished to challenge his audience's sense of values.

In terms of his craft, Steinbeck had discovered that he was most comfortable using the real language of real people, though he also hoped to demonstrate that real life is more complex than "life" as depicted in realistic art. His decision to write a novel that could be read as a play obviously helped him focus particularly on the dialogue of the characters. In a discussion of Steinbeck's stylistic technique, John Timmerman notes that "Steinbeck strove for a clipped, accurate prose. Like Ernest Hemingway (whom Steinbeck professed to have read little and comparisons with whom he disliked) Steinbeck believed that fictional prose should not be a course in 'interior decoration.' His own prose is generally marked by a spare, yeomanlike rhetoric that relies on active verbs and imagery rather than ornamentation in the pattern of James, for example."[4]

Of Mice and Men is an excellent example of the prose, stripped of decoration, that Steinbeck began to produce in his work of the 1930s. In spite of the reservations expressed by some critics about the limitations of the play-novelette form, and in light of Steinbeck's commitment to his art, he cautioned his literary agents not to make artistic compromises with publishers for the sake of financing: "Too many people are trapped into promises by gaudy offers," he wrote, and "we've gone through too damned much trying to keep the work honest and in a state of improvement to let it slip now in consideration of a little miserable popularity. I'm scared to death of popularity" (*LL,* 111).

As he began working on *Of Mice and Men,* it was clear to Steinbeck that he was more interested in being a writer than a celebrity. To his friend Ted Miller, he wrote: "My God, what a nightmare this publicity is. I don't mind being a horse's ass at all. Enjoy it in fact, but I do like to be my own kind—not that it's a better kind but it's more comfortable and I know it better" (*LL,* 131). After *Of Mice and Men* was chosen by the Book-of-the-Month Club, Steinbeck informed agent Elizabeth Otis—who worked in the same office as Mavis McIntosh—that the news was both gratifying and frightening. He claimed, "I shall never learn to conceive of money in larger quantities than two dollars. More than that has no conceptual meaning to me" (*LL,* 134). Perhaps the subject matter of the play-novella, which took him back to his earlier, more frugal years of working as a ranch hand near King City or on the Spreckels Sugar Ranches around Salinas, evoked Steinbeck's uneasiness with financial security. As Benson observes, the composition of *Of Mice and Men* "was certainly an exercise in humility. For an author who lived through the lives of his characters, [Steinbeck] was reminding himself on the gut level what it was to have nothing, truly, and very little hope for anything" (326).

Details of the writer's financial struggles in the early years of his marriage to Carol Henning underscore the authenticity of Steinbeck's interest in marginally subsistent characters with uncertain futures. John and Carol were married at the beginning of 1930, soon after the stock market crash of 1929. They had no steady income, so Steinbeck's father offered to send them $50 a month until they got on their feet. Carol and John rented a tiny shack, and John shopped in junkyards for the necessary plumbing hardware to repair the gas line and install a water heater. The rent was low, but after the young couple remodeled the place, their landlord decided it was good enough to give to his newly married son. The displaced Steinbecks finally had to settle in Pacific Grove in a summer house that belonged to John's parents. While John was writing, Carol looked for a job without much success. Many of their meals came from their fishing expeditions, their vegetable garden, or donations from friends (Benson, 165–82). Nonetheless, Steinbeck's dedication to his craft throughout the hard financial times of the early 1930s eventually paid off. The publication of *Of Mice and Men* was a benchmark in the writer's career, marking the end of his economic marginality. By the time he began working on *The Grapes of Wrath,* he knew he could make a living as a writer.

In spite of his professional achievements, artistic uncertainty plagued Steinbeck during the decade. Though there were times while he was composing *Of Mice and Men* that he judged the work to be going very well, he did not allow himself to assume success. Insisting that this book was different from anything he had written, Steinbeck referred to the manuscript as an experiment, "a tricky little thing designed to teach me to write for the theatre" (*LL,* 132). In fact, when the earliest version of the manuscript was destroyed by his dog, Steinbeck wrote to Otis that he only mildly reprimanded his pet. Maintaining that "the poor little fellow may have been acting critically," he explained, "I didn't want to ruin a good dog for a [manuscript] I'm not sure is good at all" (*LL,* 124). Because of the experimental nature of the book, Steinbeck would not allow himself to express a great deal of enthusiasm for what would prove to be one of his most read works.

With *Of Mice and Men,* Steinbeck set out to create a novella that could be performed as a play directly from the original text. He hoped that such a form would make the story more accessible to working-class people unlikely to attend theaters or read novels of the usual length and complexity. In line with this plan, the work was performed as intended by the Theatre Union in San Francisco in the spring and summer of 1937. Nevertheless, when playwright and director George Kaufman asked Steinbeck to rework the story into a script for a Broadway production, the author complied without complaint. The relative ease with which the book was transformed into a play testifies to the validity of Steinbeck's original intentions: more than 80 percent of the lines in the book went into the playscript (Timmerman, 95).

Steinbeck was breaking new ground philosophically as well as formally in writing his play-novelette. By 1936, he had become very interested in non-teleological thinking, the scientific philosophy that concentrates on the conditions of existence rather than on causes and effects of these conditions. Biologist Ed Ricketts, whom Steinbeck met in 1930, both preached and practiced his own interpretation of non-teleology. Ricketts insisted on looking at the whole picture of life and on seeing himself as part of that picture; he held an all-embracing worldview that professed a universal unity of all things. Such a philosophy is characterized by a point of view that accepts things as they are without assigning blame to individuals or situations. Though Steinbeck often described *Of Mice and Men* as something totally new and experimental, Benson recognizes several elements of the story as extensions of his previous efforts in *In Dubious Battle,* namely the presentation of a conflict "without taking sides" and "the attempt to write from a completely non-teleological standpoint: no cause and effect, no problem and solution, no heroes or villains" (327). As with *In Dubious Battle,* however, readers of *Of Mice and Men* have drawn their own conclusions about heroes and villains in the story in spite of the neutral narrative stance. As Timmerman points out, non-teleological thinking

12

does not sufficiently explain the problem of evil that presents itself in Steinbeck's fiction. He argues that

> [i]f we observe aberration in the animal world, we classify it; if we find it in the human world we ask why. Then we try to find cause and effect and remedy. Why? Because human life has will; the very fact that one wonders about the distinction between teleological or willful thinking and non-teleological or nonwillful thinking presupposes a will capable of choosing one or the other. . . . Despite its philosophical insufficiency, the theory had a profound effect on Steinbeck's artistry, particularly in the animal and vegetable imagery that roots his characters to the earth. (Timmerman, 22–23)

Nevertheless, there is no doubt that Steinbeck was influenced by Ricketts's beliefs, as evidenced in their coauthorship of *Sea of Cortez* (1941) and in Steinbeck's *The Log from the Sea of Cortez* (1951), which contains a comprehensive statement of the Ricketts/Steinbeck *is thinking,* or non-teleological, beliefs.[5]

Steinbeck and Ricketts were best friends until Ricketts's accidental death in 1948. According to Richard Astro, "[n]o analysis of Steinbeck's world view, his philosophy of life, can proceed without a careful study of the life, work, and ideas of this remarkable human being who was Steinbeck's closest personal and intellectual companion for nearly two decades" (4). The association with Ricketts helped Steinbeck to cultivate a more objective, scientific view of human nature than he had been able to achieve in his first novel, *Cup of Gold* (1929). Though he had drafted a complete manuscript for *To a God Unknown* (1933) before meeting Ricketts, Steinbeck revised the work considerably after he began to explore non-teleological thinking. The published version of the novel illustrates the futility of a mystical belief in human manipulation of natural phenomena. Joseph Wayne, the central character in *To a God Unknown,* engages in teleological thinking, attempting to change something that cannot be changed (the cycle of drought and rain in the California valley).

Trying to work within this non-teleological philosophical framework, Steinbeck originally titled *Of Mice and Men* "Something that

Happened." Nevertheless, Astro warns—and rightly so—against reading *Of Mice and Men* strictly as the fictionalization of Ricketts's brand of non-teleological thinking:

> [T]o do so would be to deny the novelist's insistence on the importance of man's voluntary acceptance of his responsibilities, which is based on his belief that man owes something to man. Viewed in perspective, what Steinbeck seems to be doing in *Of Mice and Men* is using Ricketts' ideas about non-teleological thinking not as theme, but as fictional method. He tells the story of Lennie and George from a nonblaming point of view, but never does he suggest the unimportance of the teleological considerations symbolized by Lennie's dream. (105–6)

Happily, the novel proved to be a successful marriage of form and philosophy. With the dramatic structure focusing on the characters' dialogue and actions, Steinbeck achieved a narrative intensity that is largely untainted by authorial voice.

Steinbeck may have intended only to tell a good story in *Of Mice and Men* and to cast that story into a new form; but in carrying out his experiment, he also created a situation that appears, indeed, to have causes and effects, to delineate problems that have no easy solutions—a situation in which it is easy to identify villains but not heroes. Peter Lisca, in a focused essay that looks at the theme of escape and commitment in Steinbeck's canon, emphasizes the complexities in the seemingly simple story of *Of Mice and Men* and warns against the temptation of an obvious thematic reading of the text. Lisca states that *Of Mice and Men*

> could be used to illustrate the escape theme by pointing out the persistent dream of George and Lennie to get a place of their own; and even the mercy killing of Lennie by George could be seen as providing Lennie with permanent escape from a world with which he cannot cope, into the dream of the little house and a couple of acres, and rabbits. Or, by concentrating on George, and reading Lennie as a symbol of proletarian man, great in strength but helpless without leadership, the theme of commitment could be seen in George's sacrifices and devotion to Lennie.

Or, by bringing out both of these patterns, the novelette could be made to illustrate the nice *balancing* of these two themes.[6]

Lisca goes on to reject an application of his escape and commitment theme analysis for *Of Mice and Men;* the escape is only an illusion, he says, and the commitment is questionable because "[o]n one level, Lennie is necessary to George as an excuse for his own failure" (Lisca 1971, 82). Though an uncomplicated thematic reading of the novella is problematic—an issue I take up at some length in chapter 5—it is possible to see that the dramatic action in *Of Mice and Men* carries a social message that Steinbeck went on to develop in epic proportions in *The Grapes of Wrath:* the American dream is perhaps only an illusion, but it is an illusion that can empower or destroy those who seek to attain it. While commitment to a dream for a better life may be a worthwhile investment of emotional energy, belief in the dignity of all human beings is even more important. A social system that allows for the success of some of its citizens at the expense of basic human dignity for others ultimately corrupts even those who appear to succeed.

As Warren French observes about Steinbeck's novels of the 1930s, they "continue to sell well when most of the proletarian sagas of the period are forgotten. Many readers at home and abroad have gained their strongest image of that troubled decade through Steinbeck's vivid fictional portrayal of it."[7] Sylvia Cook, whose primary interest in Steinbeck's work of the 1930s is with the Communist party influences on the fiction, also nominates Steinbeck as a major contributor of proletarian literature of the period, though she concludes that Steinbeck never intended to promote the Communist party. Cook reasons that

> there is no evidence in Steinbeck's fiction, his letters, or the outward course of his life that he underwent any dramatic conversion away from the remote, heroic, and mystical concerns of his early work to the more topical, naturalistic, and political orientation of *The Grapes of Wrath.* What there is ample evidence for is a gradual and logical evolution of the social metaphors in which Steinbeck embodied his biological interests, that caused him to

shift his focus from the marine life of the tide pools to the Communist party and thence to the Joad family. This shift was aided, not by literary ideologues in New York, but his empirical observations in California, where he spent almost the entire decade. (12)

Cook claims that Steinbeck was innocent of leftist ideology and its exploitation, an assertion with which I agree. In fact, I believe that this very ideological innocence is one reason that Steinbeck's fiction of the period has sustained its popular appeal. Moreover, a Jungian reading of the novella suggests that Steinbeck reaches the collective unconscious of many people. Readers often respond strongly to the social message in *Of Mice and Men,* to the expert craftsmanship of the narrative, or to both. Consequently, in the five decades since its publication, *Of Mice and Men* has always found an audience. Fortunately for readers of good fiction, Steinbeck did not run away after the uproar over *In Dubious Battle.* Instead of giving up, he threw himself into a virtual creative frenzy that by the end of the decade had produced *Of Mice and Men, The Long Valley,* and *The Grapes of Wrath.*

3

Critical Reception

Throughout his career, Steinbeck's perception of his reading audience may have varied depending on the subject or form of each particular work, but we can safely assume that he never wrote *for* literary critics. On several occasions, however, Steinbeck published comments *about* his critics and literary criticism in general. In "Critics—From a Writer's Viewpoint," which appeared in the *Saturday Review*, 27 August 1955, Steinbeck claimed that most critics are creative writers or want to be creative writers. Writing criticism is what the critic does to survive, "until he can become novelist, playwright, or poet and if, in the course of years, he should become none of these he must, no matter how much he may resist, develop an anger against those who do."[1]

In another piece, "A Letter on Criticism," published by the *Colorado Quarterly* on 5 February 1955, Steinbeck described literary criticism as "a kind of ill tempered parlour game in which nobody gets kissed" (Tedlock and Wicker, 52). Steinbeck argued that reading criticism of his work was of little use to him as a writer since he was not likely to rewrite a finished piece. Though Steinbeck, from the beginning of his career to the end, claimed to pay little attention to the professional audience of critics, after the sensational public response to

Tortilla Flat, literary critics nevertheless began paying attention to John Steinbeck, writer.

Perhaps because it appeared so soon after the successful *Tortilla Flat, Of Mice and Men* was favored by the best critical reception of any of Steinbeck's previously published works. Selection by the Book-of-the-Month Club guaranteed a sale of 10,000 copies. The play version opened on Broadway for the Thanksgiving season and won the New York Drama Critics' Circle Award. Undoubtedly, the success on Broadway added momentum to the initial popularity of the novella, just as subsequent film versions of the story have helped it to maintain public recognition for decades. In this chapter, however, I will focus on the responses of literary critics to the book. A summary of critical reactions to the films and the play, including the negative responses of feminist critics in the 1970s, appears in chapter 6.

Because of the obvious social messages in Steinbeck's 1930s fiction, some critics viewed the novels as tracts and overlooked their value as literature. Burton Rascoe's noteworthy discussion of *Of Mice and Men,* which appeared in the March 1938 issue of the *English Journal,* shifted the critical focus from Steinbeck's subjects to Steinbeck's craft as a writer. In "John Steinbeck," Rascoe looks at the play-novelette in light of the problems it presented to a writer: if the first five pages of the book allow a perceptive reader to predict what is likely to happen, how does a writer make the narration itself the compelling reason for reading the work to the end? Rascoe asserts that Steinbeck solved this problem "in a Sophoclean manner, that is, without poetic or rhetorical fault," by treating nature the way Greek tragedians treated characters of tragedy, subject to "the high sin of *hubris* or arrogance or insolence and its consequence" (Tedlock and Wicker, 60, 65).

Rascoe is touched by the sense of social responsibility in the story, and he admires the construction of the land-dream recitations, which run "like a Greek choral chant throughout the novel and the play, infecting, enlivening, and ennobling not only George and Lennie but the crippled, broken-down ranch hand, Candy, and the twisted-back Negro stable buck, Crooks" (Tedlock and Wicker, 61). Along this same laudatory line, Joseph Warren Beach discusses Steinbeck's work in "John Steinbeck: Journeyman Artist," which appeared as part of a longer critical study, *American Fiction: 1920–1940*. Beach compares Steinbeck favorably to Chekhov, calling Steinbeck a "literary genius" (Tedlock and Wicker, 82). Though Beach overlooks the social consciousness of *Of Mice and Men* entirely, he commends Steinbeck for the "elegant economy of words" that tantalizes the reader's imagination (Tedlock and Wicker, 82).

The earliest full-length study of Steinbeck's work appeared in 1939, just after the publication of *The Grapes of Wrath*. In *The Novels of John Steinbeck: A First Critical Study*, Harry Thornton Moore praised Steinbeck's depiction of ranch life in *Of Mice and Men*, but lamented that the book depicts "violence without tragedy," an assessment that hinges on a distinction between <u>social tragedy</u> and <u>literary tragedy</u> in the classic sense.[2] In spite of his critical reservations, however, Moore predicted that "the author of *Of Mice and Men* is in vogue now: in America, those in vogue can do little wrong. The vogue will last as long as Steinbeck can hold the public's interest; eventually he may be displaced by writers whom the public will consider more interesting, but such a day seems at this time, very remote" (96). This comment by Moore points to a critical bias that Steinbeck faced throughout his career: the tendency of academic critics to belittle the literary value of works that appeal to the broad reading public, a critical snobbery, if you will.

The same tone permeates Alfred Kazin's discussion of Steinbeck's work in the definitive study *On Native Grounds* (1942). Kazin, after giving Steinbeck credit for being a social realist "who did promise something different from the automatism of contemporary naturalism and the cult of the hard-boiled," praises *The Grapes of Wrath* as "tonic sanity in a bad time."[3] Then, to ensure that the academy not accuse him of embracing a popular author, Kazin sharply criticizes Steinbeck for the sterile "moral serenity" in *Of Mice and Men*, which was responsible for the "calculated sentimentality" of the story (309).

Edwin Berry Burgum's "The Sensibility of John Steinbeck," first published in the spring 1946 issue of *Science and Society*, echoes Kazin's complaints. Burgum writes: "Although always remaining of benevolent intention [Steinbeck] swung in his various novels from the extreme of a deep and legitimate admiration for working people to that in which all values are paralyzed in the apathy of the sentimental" (Tedlock and Wicker, 104). Burgum, however, recognizes Steinbeck's skills in characterization and praises his handling of "the difficult relationship between George and Lenny [*sic*]" (Tedlock and Wicker, 110). He then tempers his early accusation of sentimentality by admitting in the conclusion of his discussion of *Of Mice and Men* that Steinbeck is able to arouse awe without resorting to mysticism by leaving Lennie "somehow entirely natural and human, and yet essentially a mystery, the mystery of the unfit in a practical world" (Tedlock and Wicker, 112).

Though critics like Burgum tried to render a balanced view of Steinbeck's work, a simplistic glibness characterizes much of the critical commentary in the late 1940s and early 1950s, especially in relation to the notions of Steinbeck's naturalism and sentimentalism. For example, Freeman Champney, in "John Steinbeck, Californian," which appeared in the fall 1947 issue of *Antioch Review*, remarked that "*Of Mice and Men* is little else besides a variation of the theme 'every man kills the thing he loves'" (Tedlock and Wicker, 140). John S. Kennedy, in "John Steinbeck: Life Affirmed and Dissolved," which first appeared in 1951 as a chapter of *Fifty Years of the American Novel*, declares that "Steinbeck's preoccupation with life and living is perhaps the main reason for his popularity and influence. . . . He can be acutely sensitive and true for a chapter, then embarrassingly sentimental and cheaply trite" (Tedlock and Wicker, 120). Statements like those made by Champney and Kennedy can be attributed to the same critical elitism that colors the discussions of Moore and Kazin.

Almost 20 years after *Of Mice and Men* first appeared, *Modern Fiction Studies* published a bold essay by Peter Lisca, "Motif and Pattern in *Of Mice and Men*." Lisca points out that "critics who saw nothing beyond the obvious plot disliked the work immensely. Those who suspected more important levels of meaning were unable to offer specific and thorough explication."[4] He then offers his own specific and thorough explication of what he calls the "three incremental motifs: symbol, action, and language" in *Of Mice and Men* (Lisca 1956, 228). Lisca later incorporated much of this discussion into his influential book *The Wide World of John Steinbeck*. Responding to what, in his estimation, had been two decades of myopic criticism of Steinbeck's writing, Lisca introduces this 1981 study with the following observation:

> John Steinbeck's literary reputation continues to suffer from a body of criticism whose assumptions were established on the first three of his novels to receive serious attention and whose prejudices have obscured the very considerable accomplishment of his fiction. Coming as they did near the end of the Great Depression and dealing with proletarian materials, it was inevitable that *In Dubious Battle* (1936), *Of Mice and Men* (1937), and *The Grapes of Wrath* (1939) should have been both accepted and rejected on sociological rather than aesthetic terms.[5]

Lisca's work goes a long way toward correcting the inadequacies of previous critics who failed to understand the craftsmanship of Steinbeck's fiction. In his discussion of *Of Mice and Men*, Lisca concentrates on the recurring motifs mentioned above (language, action, and symbol) that contribute to the sense of inevitable failure of the land dream. Recognizing a countermovement of hope in the story that produces dramatic tension, Lisca praises Steinbeck's ability to compose a pattern of events that is neither trite nor mechanical (Lisca 1981, 140–42).

Richard Astro's discussion of the novella in *John Steinbeck and Edward F. Ricketts: The Shaping of a Novelist* also focuses on strengths of craftsmanship. Like Lisca, Astro warns readers against critical attempts to limit discussion of the book to thematic arguments; he insists that what is most important about *Of Mice and Men* is "Steinbeck's uniquely delicate handling of his fictional materials, which accounts for the book's particular excellence" (105).

Echoing the concerns of Lisca and Astro is William Goldhurst in "*Of Mice and Men*: John Steinbeck's Parable of the Curse of Cain," which first appeared in the summer 1971 issue of *Western American Literature*. Goldhurst remarks on two significant aspects of the varied critical commentary on *Of Mice and Men*: first, its testament to the "inherent fertility" of the work itself, which "has furnished two generations of readers with material for intellectual sustenance," and second, its omission of any consideration of "the religious sources of *Of Mice and Men* and its mythical-allegorical implications."[6] Goldhurst constructed a detailed, convincing reading of the novella as Steinbeck's early variation on "the symbol story of the human soul"—the biblical story of Cain and Abel (51). Years after writing *Of Mice and Men,* Steinbeck wrote a much longer, more complex work around this very theme in *East of Eden* (1952).

Though Goldhurst's evaluation of *Of Mice and Men* suggested layers of meaning and a complexity not previously perceived, other critics continued to have difficulty recognizing the work as a masterpiece because of its stark simplicity. Howard Levant, in *The Novels of John Steinbeck: A Critical Study* (1974), considered *Of Mice and Men,* along with *The Moon Is Down* (1942) and *Burning Bright* (1950), in a chapter devoted to Steinbeck's play-novelettes. Levant asserts that Steinbeck's insistence on the form of the play-novelette limits the development of the story to physical action and the development of theme to parable. Reasoning that "it is impossible to handle complex human motives and relationships within those limits," Levant concluded that *Of Mice and Men* was only a "simple anecdote."[7] The logical fallacy in such an assessment is clear: if we were to take Levant seriously here, we would have to conclude that drama as a form is inherently flawed and that any play that focuses on physical action is merely "a simple anecdote."

A more favorable, though still rather narrow, assessment of *Of Mice and Men* was presented by Warren French in the revised edition of *John Steinbeck.* French identifies Steinbeck's "best works" as "those in which self-conscious characters transcend the frustrations of their environments—*The Red Pony, The Grapes of Wrath, Cannery Row*" (French 1975, 173). He classifies *Of Mice and Men* along with *The Pastures of Heaven* and a few short stories as Steinbeck's "next best works," those in which he "presents the pathetic defeats of Naturalistic characters" (French 1975, 173). French stresses the connection between naturalistic and non-teleological points of view and judges Steinbeck's work in the 1930s to be "the most remarkable and consistent body of Naturalistic writing in American literature" (French 1975, 87).

Critical Reception

For five decades, *Of Mice and Men* survived charges of animalism, sentimentalism, melodrama, and trite social protest. In the 1980s, scholars of American literature began making substantial claims for Steinbeck's achievements that go far beyond Warren French's praise for him as a naturalistic writer. Louis Owens, in *John Steinbeck's Re-Vision of America* (1985), asserts, "Though he did not always achieve the artistic craftsmanship of *The Grapes of Wrath* or the clarity of the shorter novels (*In Dubious Battle, Tortilla Flat, Of Mice and Men, Cannery Row*), Steinbeck's entire body of fiction nonetheless represents a single-minded attempt to come to grips with the idea of America, an attempt comparable in its intensity and scope to that of such great predecessors as Melville, Hawthorne, and James."[8] Owens's study carefully uncovers Steinbeck's efforts "to awaken America to the failure at the heart of the American Dream and provide an alternative to that dream" (Owens, 3). According to Owens, Steinbeck's alternative to the flawed vision of America as Eden is an ideal of commitment to humankind and to the environment, a holistic reverence for life. In this light, *Of Mice and Men* emerges as a skillfully rendered dramatization of the precepts to which Steinbeck dedicated his life's work.

In another important study, *John Steinbeck's Fiction: The Aesthetics of the Road Taken* (1986), John H. Timmerman argues that *Of Mice and Men* "achieves an artistic richness of structure and theme that ranks it among the best of [Steinbeck's] works" (96). As Timmerman's title suggests, he is especially interested in the craft, and he is particularly impressed by the "framing and foreshadowing . . . the development of Lennie's character and the theme of friendship" and by Steinbeck's exploration of "the nature of human dreams" (96). What Timmerman comes back to, it seems, is a full explanation of the issue raised by Burton Rascoe almost 50 years earlier—Steinbeck's aesthetic skill.

In concluding this brief overview of the book's critical reception, it is encouraging to note that Viking Press has just issued a new edition of *Of Mice and Men* and that the novella continues to sell to general readers as well as to high school and college students all over the world. As I add to the large body of discussion devoted to both the form and the content of this slim masterpiece, my intention is to perform a valuable service for the novella's many readers. Nevertheless, even as I write, I realize that Steinbeck has already performed the most valuable service of all to lovers of good literature by creating *Of Mice and Men*. Therefore, it seems appropriate to allow him to have the last word in this chapter on critical commentary. In 1955, the editor of *Colorado Quarterly* invited Steinbeck to comment on two essays about *The Grapes of Wrath* that had appeared in the journal. Steinbeck's rather terse response, "A Letter on Criticism," includes this statement: "Please believe me when I say I have nothing against the scholarly or critical approach. It does seem to me to have very little to do with writing or reading books" (Tedlock and Wicker, 53).

Read this to the students, sometime

A READING

4

An Experiment in Form

In the earliest stages of the writing experiment that would develop into *Of Mice and Men*, Steinbeck compared the thrill of literary experimentation to the "kind of excitement like that you get near a dynamo from breathing pure oxygen." He explained: "This work is going quickly and should get done quickly. I'm using a new set of techniques as far as I know but I am so ill read that it may have been done. Not that that matters at all, except that the unexplored in method makes the job at once more difficult because I can't tell what it will get over and more pleasant because it requires more care. I'm not interested in method as such but I am interested in having a vehicle exactly adequate to the theme" (*LL*, 124).

The vehicle Steinbeck crafted for *Of Mice and Men* was a form he called a play-novelette, a novel that could be read as such but could also be performed on stage by working directly from the text. Each section of the book is a clearly focused episode in which Steinbeck evokes the natural elements of sunlight, shade, and darkness to convey a sense of stage lighting and the opening and closing of scenes. Just as in his prize-winning short story "The Murder," each of the six chapters or sections of the novella begins with the physical details of the scene as the author sets the stage for the dramatic action that will follow.[1]

In the first paragraph of the book, our attention is drawn to the sunlight on the river; the water slips over the sand before reaching the pool in the grove where we will eventually meet George and Lennie. Once Steinbeck has shown us the valley in full light, he narrows the perspective to focus on the grove: "The shade climbed up the hills toward the top. . . . And then from the direction of the state highway came the sound of footsteps on crisp sycamore leaves . . . and then two men emerged from the path and came into the opening by the green pool."[2] In this excerpt, the clear, descriptive prose, though perfectly suited to the events of the narrative, can also be read as stage directions. The entire first scene takes place in the grove, with most of the action centered around the campfire. The episode closes as "the red light dimmed on the coals." With the fading light, we are given details of sound effects: "Up the hill from the river a coyote yammered, and a dog answered from the other side of the stream. The sycamore leaves whispered in a little night breeze" (*OMM*, 16).

Part 2 opens with physical details of setting so specific that a set designer could recreate the scene on stage with no further instructions; the prop crew would need no imagination whatsoever to furnish the room. Steinbeck mentions the shape of the bunkhouse, the number of square windows, the woodstove, the square table with boxes for chairs, the wooden latch on the door. There are eight bunks, "five of them made up with blankets and the other three showing their burlap ticking. Over each bunk there was nailed an apple box with the opening forward so that it made two shelves for the personal belongings of the occupant of the bunk" (*OMM*, 17). Even the items on the shelves are mentioned. The position of the morning sun, which "threw a bright dust-laden bar through one of the side windows" (*OMM*, 17–18), signals the rising curtain.

All of part 2 takes place in this room where entrances and exits are announced, and new characters are introduced by their physical appearances, just as George and Lennie had been described in the opening scene. The action begins with the raising of the wooden latch on the bunkhouse door and the entrance of Candy, George, and

Lennie. As in part 1, the stage is set and then the principal characters enter. The tension of the story line increases throughout the scene each time the wooden latch is raised or some new character steps into the doorway. The ranch boss comes in, questions George and Lennie, complains about their tardiness, and leaves. He is soon followed by his son Curley, who does the same. Sensing trouble, George reminds Lennie to hide in the grove if anything bad happens. Lennie has just finished rehearsing his directions when Curley's wife enters, literally casting a shadow on a thematically darkening scene. Steinbeck writes: "Both men glanced up, for the rectangle of sunshine in the doorway was cut off. A girl was standing there looking in" (*OMM*, 31). Steinbeck describes the woman, her attire, and the details of her makeup as she stands there, framed by the doorway, the sunlight coming into the room from behind her.

Walking into the light behind Curley's wife is Slim; she speaks to him and leaves, but his entrance is delayed until after George's warning to Lennie to stay away from the woman. Just as the negative energy of the situation seems to have reached a breaking point, Slim enters, freshly washed up for dinner, bringing with him an air of sanity and fairness. Again, the character description reads like stage directions:

> A tall man stood in the doorway. He held a crushed Stetson hat under his arm while he combed his long black, damp hair straight back. Like the others he wore blue jeans and a short denim jacket. When he had finished combing his hair he moved into the room, and he moved with a majesty only achieved by royalty and master craftsmen. He was a jerkline skinner, the prince of the ranch. . . . His authority was so great that his word was taken on any subject, be it politics or love. (*OMM*, 33)

Slim's presence breaks the tension that George created in his ominous words to Lennie. By drawing George into a conversation about work and fellowship, Slim gives George an opportunity to compliment Lennie's strength. Approving of the rare partnership between his two new workers, Slim, whom Steinbeck has introduced as a benevolent authority, sanctions the union between George and Lennie.

Carlson, another barley bucker, enters next and brings up the subject of Slim's dog, who has just had a litter of puppies. Lennie becomes excited on hearing about the puppies, but the mood darkens again as Carlson details his plan for getting rid of Candy's old dog. George and Lennie head for the doorway to exit the bunkhouse, but just as they reach it Curley bounces in, looking for his wife. This chance encounter prefigures the serious encounter between Lennie, George, and Curley at the end of part 3. The scene closes with everyone leaving the bunkhouse, where "the sunshine lay in a thin line under the window" (*OMM*, 37). Candy's old dog, whose death sentence has already been pronounced by Carlson, limps into the room and drops to the floor. Steinbeck juxtaposes the dog's lethargy and Curley's restlessness by giving us one more glimpse of Curley, who "popped into the doorway again and stood looking at the room" (*OMM*, 37).

By the end of part 2, Steinbeck has introduced all of the characters and major conflicts of the story. Part 3 begins with stage and lighting directions: "Although there was evening brightness showing through the windows of the bunkhouse, inside it was dusk" (*OMM*, 38). Enter Slim and George. Using dialogue as exposition, Steinbeck economically fills in the narrative gaps between scenes while continuing to advance the plot. As Slim and George converse, we learn that Slim has given Lennie one of his puppies—a simple gesture that has multiple ramifications in terms of plot and theme development: George's gratitude and friendship toward Slim, further demonstration of Lennie's lack of control, more pressure on Candy to give up his old dog. The discussion between George and Slim about Lennie and the trouble he got into in Weed sheds light on the past and foreshadows the future. As the two men talk, periodically the narrative eye monitors the progress of time from early evening to darkness by noting the intensity of light coming through the windows of the bunkhouse. Candy enters when it is almost dark outside. Then, "the thick-bodied Carlson came in out of the darkening yard. He walked to the other end of the bunkhouse and turned on the second shaded light" (*OMM*, 44).

But the artificial lights of the room cannot expel the dark mood that has entered with Candy and Carlson. While George, Slim, and

Each Part begins w/ stage & lighting directions.

30

Whit, another barley bucker, sit by silently, Carlson coerces Candy into letting him take the old dog out to shoot him. After the sound of the pistol breaks the tension, the scene is busy with numerous exits and entrances, punctuated by the pivotal conversation between George, Lennie, and Candy, in which the old man offers his life savings to George for a partnership in the farm George and Lennie plan to buy. For a moment, the dream of escaping the migrant worker's life seems to be within the realm of reality. The hopeful mood is quickly cut short, however, when Curley enters the bunkhouse. Thinking that Lennie is laughing at him, Curley attacks Lennie, and Lennie crushes his hand at George's command. The trouble George has been anticipating is just beginning, and there is no neat "curtain closing" on this scene. Slim makes Curley promise not tell his father what has happened, and then Curley is taken off to the hospital. George and Lennie are left alone in the room, and the scene ends.

Part 4 begins with a close-up of the room in the barn occupied by Crooks, the black stable hand, which is described in the same meticulous manner as the bunkhouse had been. Crooks's interlude with Lennie, though it seems to provide a lull in the physical action of the plot, develops Lennie's character further and reinforces the theme of the illusory land dream. With the introduction of Curley's wife into the scene, and the emphasis upon her interest in Lennie as the person who injured Curley's hand, Steinbeck sets the stage for the dramatic conclusion of the story. Part 5, the last episode of the story to take place on the ranch, is also set in the barn and opens with Lennie's lament over his dead puppy. Alone in the barn, he talks to himself, expressing his fear that George will be angry. He tries to decide if his accidental killing of the puppy should be considered a bad thing, meaning he should go hide in the grove by the pool. This is the first time Lennie has the "stage" to himself, and Steinbeck uses this moment to illustrate how truly dangerous Lennie is: he possesses tremendous physical strength over which he has no control, and he depends entirely on George to think for him.

Lennie's conversation with his dead puppy resembles a tragic hero's soliloquy in which he reveals to the audience his mind, his heart, and the motives for his actions. Lennie, however, instead of being a tragic hero, is simply a tragedy of nature, for we can clearly see he has no control over his mind, his heart, or his actions. Curley's wife, who meets her death at Lennie's hands, acts as a character foil for Lennie in this scene. Her gender appears to be a tragedy of nature as well: because she is a woman in a man's world, she has little or no control over her life; and because she has no understanding whatsoever of Lennie's power and lack of control, she loses her life in an instant. Instinctively, before fleeing for the sycamore grove by the river, Lennie covers the woman's dead body with hay, just as he had covered the dead puppy. Moments later, she is discovered, and the lynch mob is off in pursuit of Lennie.

The final episode brings us to the same setting, even the same time of day, as the opening scene. In the quiet grove where George and Lennie first entered the story, Steinbeck brings them together again for the last time. The day is ending; shortly before George shoots Lennie, Steinbeck returns to the light/shadow motif of the first three sections of the novella. He writes: "Only the topmost ridges were in the sun now. The shadow in the valley was blue and soft" (*OMM*, 103). This description typifies the narrative passages throughout *Of Mice and Men*.

Rarely does the narrative voice break from this descriptive mode. With his decision to write a novel that could be performed as a play, Steinbeck imposed rigid restrictions on the narrative discourse and thrust all of the responsibility for exposition and plot advancement onto the dialogue and action of the characters. Thus the reader hears and sees the story unfold. Significant actions of the story—Lennie's crushing Curley's hand and his accidental killing of the puppy and of Curley's wife—fall into place alongside the seemingly insignificant details of everyday ranch life. These various misfortunes have a cumulative effect; they add up, and finally the pace of the narrative slows at the most intense moment, when George shoots Lennie by the river. The effectiveness of this dramatic technique accounts in part for the enduring success of *Of Mice and Men*. In carrying out his literary experiment, Steinbeck was able to capture some of his own excitement in the pages of this popular American classic.

5

Layers of Complexities:
Reality, Symbol, and Myth

As has been pointed out earlier in this study, all of Steinbeck's stories about California farmworkers include realistic details gleaned from the writer's experiences as an agricultural laborer and from his journalistic investigations of farm labor conditions. Descriptions of the landscape, the use of actual place names (such as Weed and Soledad in *Of Mice and Men*), the language of the men in the bunkhouse, the details of everday life (for example, the horseshoe matches and the trips to town on payday)—all contribute to the realistic impression of *Of Mice and Men*.

Steinbeck nevertheless did not consider himself a realist. In analyzing the author as a literary artist, Timmerman concludes that "[w]hile it is true that much of Steinbeck's fiction was nurtured by firsthand experience, that experience is transmuted by the artist into a thematic or spiritual experience common to humankind. Realistic in origin, by artistry Steinbeck's storytelling approaches the realism of the human spirit in much the same way, for example, that Faulkner's fiction does—by exploring the enduring questions of the nature of humanity, of good and evil, of tragedy and triumph" (Timmerman, 8–9).

Steinbeck's fictional range thus extends beyond a strict classification of realism; we come closer to understanding his aesthetic principles by examining his tendency to mine sources for convincing detail and then construct metaphors around this detail (Benson, 304).

A central metaphor in Steinbeck's work is that of America as an imperfect New World, a Garden of Eden; with this motif in mind, Steinbeck appropriated idyllic, pastoral settings for much of his fiction. In a letter to his agent Mavis McIntosh, Steinbeck identified the setting for the stories in *The Pastures of Heaven* (1932) as a valley about 12 miles from Monterey called Corral de Tierra (*LL,* 42). To his friend George Albee, Steinbeck announced his intention to represent "the valley of the world" in *The Long Valley* stories (*LL,* 73). Commenting on Steinbeck's preference for setting stories in "small confined valleys," Benson notes that "the California Coastal valley seems to suggest to [Steinbeck] a dramatic climax to the American Eden myth, a last chance for paradise at the end of the frontier."[1] Moreover, as Owens asserts in *John Steinbeck's Re-Vision of America,* the California valley setting dictates that the stories "will take place in a fallen world and that the quest for the illusive and illusory Eden will be of central thematic significance" (100).

As further background for my analysis of the Eden motif in *Of Mice and Men,* I would like to look back in Steinbeck's canon at one of those early valley stories, a selection from *The Pastures of Heaven,* which involves a mentally deficient character, Hilda Van Deventer, and her caretaker/mother, Helen. Just as George aims to contain Lennie's destructive power by retreating with him to an Edenic dream farm, Helen seeks to control her violent daughter by imprisoning her in a walled garden. In both cases, the caretakers are particularly watchful of the sexual awareness of their physically powerful, mentally deficient charges. Thus Steinbeck emphasizes sexual innocence in a prelapsarian Eden, which, according to the Genesis myth, is impossible to maintain if the history of the world is to continue. Such is the case with Steinbeck's characters, who learn that going back to the garden is impossible. Meanwhile, these characters come to see their predicaments as having only either/or solutions: in the end, both George and Helen fail to maintain control of their situations and finally resort to killing their dangerous wards in order to "protect" them. Though Steinbeck imposes no narrative judgments on the ethics of such drastic measures to preserve innocence, the stories themselves raise ethical questions.

In the *Pastures of Heaven* story, as in *Of Mice and Men,* Steinbeck develops the two central characters as opposites, though Jungian overtones of self and shadow self (discussed in detail later in this chapter) are apparent in both stories. Helen Van Deventer, Steinbeck tells us, shrouds herself in sorrow from the time she is 15 years old. She mourns her kitten's death until her father dies six months later; then her "mourning continued uninterrupted."[2] Life, it seems, obliges Helen's hunger for tragedy, and her husband dies in a hunting accident three months after the wedding. Helen does not weep for her loss; instead, she "closed off the drawing room with its [hunting] trophies. Thereafter the room was holy to the spirit of Hubert."

Six months later, Helen has a baby girl, Hilda, "a pretty, doll-like baby, with her mother's great eyes" (*PH,* 65). Hilda's destructive, angry temperament, however, is the antithesis of Helen's controlled, restrained personality, and the mother's calmness only fuels the child's anger. Steinbeck explains that Helen's attempts to soothe and pet her child only succeed in increasing her temper. When Hilda is six years old, her doctor informs Helen that the child is mentally ill. With Helen's response to this announcement, Steinbeck prepares us for the subsequent development of Hilda's personality. Helen immediately blames herself for Hilda's illness by claiming "I didn't have the strength to bear a perfect child." She then rejects all of the doctor's suggestions for professional help, insisting that she will keep Hilda with her always, and "no one else must interfere" (*PH,* 66). George's decision to keep Lennie with him instead of allowing him to be institutionalized reflects a similar penchant for martyrdom.

Because of their decisions to become caretakers of potentially dangerous people, both Helen and George isolate themselves from productive interaction with others. Helen's case is more extreme than George's: she worships daily at the shrine of her dead husband as she nurtures a violent, mentally disturbed child who symbolizes her own repressed emotional and sexual self. Throughout the story, Steinbeck subtly draws attention to the symbolic role of Helen's daughter. As I will demonstrate later, Lennie serves a similar symbolic role in terms of George's psychological needs.

Hilda, for example, suffers from visions and dreams of "terrible creatures of the night, with claws and teeth," and "ugly little men" who "pinched her and gritted their teeth in her ear" (*PH*, 67). Such visions function as parallel, but contrasting, manifestations of Helen's ritual hour in Hubert's trophy room, during which she "practiced a dream that was pleasure to her" (*PH*, 76). By staring at the mounted trophies—controlled, subdued versions of Hilda's nightmare creatures—Helen evokes Hubert's presence. Helen appears to have control over the phenomena of dreams. Just as she sits at Hilda's bedside all night to banish the nightmare creatures, Helen also practices banishing the creature of her own dreams: "She built up [Hubert's] image until it possessed the room and filled it with the surging vitality of the great hunter. Then, when she had completed the dream, she smashed it" (*PH*, 77).

Similarly, George controls Lennie's dreams by teaching him to recite the dream-farm litany. George himself brings our attention to his role as controller of Lennie's thoughts when he tells Slim that Lennie "can't think of nothing to do himself, but he sure can take orders" (*OMM*, 39), a remark that reveals George's naïveté. Though George can put words into Lennie's mouth, can even silence Lennie when he chooses, his control over Lennie's physical actions is tenuous.

Helen Van Deventer suffers from the same illusion of control. When Helen suspects that Hilda has made contact with the world beyond her garden because the child proudly shows her a wristwatch that she claims was a gift from an old man, the mother is horrified. Steinbeck writes: Helen "crept into the garden, found a trowel and buried the watch deep in the earth. That week she had a high iron fence built around the garden and Hilda was never permitted to go out alone after that" (*PH*, 68). Helen's burying the watch and installing the fence underscore her delusive drive to stop time, resist change, and return to an innocent Eden. In spite of Helen's efforts, when Hilda reaches puberty, she becomes even more difficult to restrain. The girl runs away for four days, is found by the police, and then tells her mother that she "was married to a young gypsy man" and that she was "going to have a little baby" (*PH*, 68).

Even though the doctor affirms Helen's suspicion that Hilda is lying about the gypsy man, Helen decides to move to a new place. Consequently, she builds a log cabin and retreats even further from life by taking Hilda to Christmas Canyon. The name of the place evokes Christian associations of new life, a chance for salvation—Helen's apparent reasons for moving; but Steinbeck undercuts these positive expectations with Helen's insistence that the yard appear as "an old garden" (*PH*, 71) and with the comment that Christmas Canyon is "not a place to farm" (*PH*, 73). These details point to Helen's quest for an illusion of Eden, a quest that renders her life sterile. By isolating Hilda in an enclosed garden to protect her virginity, Helen acts out the inner drama of repressing her own sexual urges and denying herself the opportunity to fulfill natural physical and emotional desires.

But retreating further into an illusion of paradise does not placate Hilda; in a screaming rage, she declares, "I won't ever like it here, ever," and then "she plucked a garden stick from the ground and struck her mother across the breast with it" (*PH*, 72). Nor does the retreat to paradise eliminate Helen's unarticulated need to overcome her morbid self-repression. On the first night in Christmas Canyon, Helen plans to "welcome her dream" of Hubert "into its new home," but while she is walking in the garden she experiences a sense of release from her tragic history; she feels as if she is "looking forward to something," and "all of a sudden Helen realized that she didn't want to think of Hubert any more" (*PH*, 79–80). Apparently, while Helen is experiencing this sensation of release, Hilda is plotting her own escape from repression. When the two meet at dinner, "all traces of the afternoon's rage were gone from Hilda's face; she looked happy, and very satisfied with herself" (*PH*, 80). When Helen comments on her daughter's pleasant demeanor, Hilda announces her plan to run away and get married.

Ironically, Helen muses that her daughter's story is just another of her fantasies. Then the mother engages in her own fantasy. To rid herself of Hubert, she must confront him directly. She discovers that "when her mind dropped his hands they disappeared," and she was free from Hubert's presence for the first time since his death. The expectancy she had experienced earlier returns to her as she opens the windows, drinks in the night air, and enjoys the sounds of life coming from the garden and beyond. While the mother is experiencing this emotional, spiritual release, Hilda is sawing through one of the oaken bars on her bedroom window and escaping from the house. By representing these scenes as simultaneous occurrences, Steinbeck emphasizes Hilda's symbolic role as a physical representation of her mother's spiritual state. A similar juxtaposition of events occurs in *Of Mice and Men:* George is participating in a game of horseshoes with the rest of the ranch hands, enjoying himself, and just being one of the guys, while Lennie, close by in the barn, is having his fatal encounter with Curley's wife—the incident that leads to Lennie's destruction and George's freedom to become like all the other ranch hands.

Just as George kills Lennie when it appears that retreating with him from the world of everyday life is no longer possible, Helen kills Hilda upon realizing that she can no longer restrain her daughter. When Helen shoots Hilda in the garden she is killing, symbolically, that part of herself that has rebelled against her naturally morbid, sterile personality and has almost escaped the boundaries of her control. Steinbeck allows Hilda's doctor, as he affirms the coroner's verdict of suicide, to articulate, unknowingly, the allegorical interpretation of the story: he concludes that a girl like Hilda "might have committed suicide or murder, depending on the circumstances" (*PH*, 84). Only the reader knows "the circumstances"—that Hilda has committed neither murder nor suicide, but that her mother has, in a sense, committed both acts simultaneously. As Melanie Mortlock notes in her allegorical reading of *The Pastures of Heaven*, "[w]ith the murder of her daughter, Helen feeds her voracious appetite for self-pity and Old Testament guilt. Because she has fancied herself to be a victim, she inevitably becomes a victimizer, and creates the situation she wants and needs to believe in, the one which permits her 'the strength to endure.'"[3]

By shooting Hilda, Helen proves to herself what she has "always suspected" (*PH*, 84): she is capable of whatever measure is required to maintain her delicious martyrdom and to purge her cloistral garden from the temptation of happiness. George's motives for killing Lennie and what he gains by Lennie's death cannot be explained as easily since the narrator offers no introspective clues on the subject. Critical discussions of the novella have generally avoided thorough analysis of George's final actions and have appeared to accept Slim's cryptic pronouncement, "You hadda, George. I swear you hadda" (*OMM,* 107). In my analysis of the work, I hope to fill this critical gap by questioning the inevitability of the novella's final scene.

Looking at the *Pastures of Heaven* helps us see more clearly how in *Of Mice and Men,* as in his other California stories, Steinbeck consciously manipulates the thematic association between the realistic valley setting and the mythical implications of the Garden of Eden story. Other forms of symbolism also figure strongly within this mythic framework. The allusive title, *Of Mice and Men,* is taken from a Robert Burns poem:

> But, Mousie, thou art no thy lane,
> In proving foresight may be vain:
> The best laid schemes o' mice and men
> Gang aft a-gley
> An' lea'e us nought but grief an' pain
> For promis'd joy.

Thus, from the outset of the novel, Steinbeck signals that mice are symbols for inevitable failure. And even before the central "scheme" of the story is delineated specifically, Steinbeck connects both central characters with mice: George is described as "small and quick, dark of face, with restless eyes and sharp, strong features" (*OMM,* 2); Lennie carries a dead mouse in his pocket because he loves to pet soft, furry things. Consequently, Lennie associates mice with the plan of owning the farm and keeping rabbits, which, unlike the mice, will be able to survive his petting them. For Lennie, the rabbits, and by extension all soft, furry things, represent the Edenic dream farm. (Lisca 1981, 136). Steinbeck's introduction of a dead mouse—a soft, furry thing—into the opening scene of the story thus signifies the ultimate destruction of the dream.

Is this a fair characterization?

In this symbolic system, Curley's wife, like the mouse and later the puppy, is simply another nice-to-touch object that is doomed when touched by Lennie. Her death is just the "something" that was bound to happen to shatter George and Lennie's plan for escaping from their transitory existence as migrant workers (Lisca 1981, 136–38). Of course, mythically and symbolically, Curley's wife fulfils the role of Woman in the Eden story, as that of the temptress, the despoiler of paradise. That Steinbeck manipulates the raw material of his story to encompass the mythic interpretation is clear. In a *New York Times* interview in December 1937, Steinbeck, while discussing his sources for characters and incidents in *Of Mice and Men,* claimed that he had witnessed Lennie's real-life counterpart kill a man, not a woman:

> "I was bindle-stiff myself for quite a spell," [Steinbeck] said. "I worked in the same country that the story is laid in. The charac-ters are composites to a certain extent. Lennie was a real person. He's in an insane asylum in California right now. I worked alongside him for many weeks. He didn't kill a girl. He killed a ranch foreman. Got sore because the boss had fired his pal and stuck a pitchfork right through his stomach. I hate to tell you how many times. I saw him do it. We couldn't stop him until it was too late."[4]

To satisfy the mythic framework of his story, then, Steinbeck makes the woman the instrument of destruction of the land dream, although the illusion of an escape to an Edenic existence would have been shat-tered just as surely if Lennie had killed Curley, for instance, instead of Curley's wife.

By thrusting a lonely woman into the society of unsophisticated working men and assigning her a destructive mythic role, Steinbeck may also have been recycling material from a much earlier story, "Fingers of Cloud," published in the *Stanford Spectator* in 1924. In Steinbeck's biography, Benson comments on the lively descriptions in this story, the realistic dialogue of the workers, and the authenticity of the bunkhouse scene as suggestive of Steinbeck's future mastery of his craft (Benson, 39, 62). The story also sheds some light on Steinbeck's early interest in the mythic characterization of women. Although the story is by all accounts inferior to *Of Mice and Men,* it is particularly relevant to my analysis of Curley's wife. In "Fingers of Cloud," an 18-year-old orphaned albino girl, Gertie, wanders away from her house and gets lost in a severe thunderstorm. She is taken in by a Filipino work gang in an isolated bunkhouse on a sugar beet ranch in the central valley of California. She becomes the wife of the gang leader, Pedro. Not surprisingly, her presence causes trouble among the workers; Pedro beats Gertie to demonstrate to everyone that he is still in charge, and finally she leaves him. Like Curley's wife, Gertie is considered to be Pedro's prize as well as his nemesis. Like Lennie, she is an aberration of nature, an albino.

At the height of the storm that brings the principal characters together, when the men hear Gertie's cry for help, Steinbeck writes: "The cry came again. It had the far-off quality of a coyote's yap as it rose and fell. Slowly it came out of the wind, shrieked up to the kill cry of a creature half woman, half lioness, and ended in the sound of water gurgling down a drain pipe."[5] The men are frightened, and the oldest Filipino warns Pedro not to open the door. "It is the Kari, Pedro—," he says. "She eats the wet brains of the new-buried dead and she crazes those who see her—Pedro, I command you not to go" ("FC," 162). Similarly, in *Of Mice and Men* all of the ranch workers (except Slim) seem to be a bit frightened of Curley's wife; old Candy warns George that she is a troublemaker, and George forms a negative opinion of the woman before he ever sees her.

Parallels between the sexual dynamics of the novella and the short story are clear. The young woman in *Of Mice and Men* marries Curley not because she is in love with him or even sexually attracted to him but simply because her choices are limited. From the story she tells Lennie in the barn, we can surmise that she has had little experience with men. In fact, she is still filled with adolescent rage against her mother for refusing to let her go to Hollywood with an actor she had met in Salinas when she was 15. When Curley proposes to her, no doubt she is impressed with his status as the ranch owner's son and his reputation as a boxer. Marriage to him seems like an attractive alternative to living with a mother who constantly discourages her from thinking about a Hollywood career. Nevertheless, the "respect" she receives at the ranch degenerates quickly into resentment, and once Curley has proven his manhood by marrying her, he appears to neglect her.

Gertie, in "Fingers of Cloud," not only is inexperienced but also seems to be feebleminded. She has no home life whatsoever, as both of her parents are dead. When she stumbles into the bunkhouse on the night of the storm, Pedro is the one who is brave enough to open the door and face the "Kari." When she washes the mud from her face and the men see that she is white, Pedro is attracted to her, offers her his room, and then boasts to the other workers that he will make her his wife. Gertie has little to say in the matter, but, for a while at least, she appears to enjoy her status as Pedro's woman. When the other men begin to show that they dislike her, Pedro also mistreats her. Her mythic power as a Kari fades quickly.

The "Kari," or "Karei," is the god of thunder to a Negrito people of the Malay Peninsula. Kari is a creator of humankind, soul-giver, and punisher of sins—particularly sexual sins and cruelty to animals. In this case, Steinbeck takes liberties with the mythic references from which he is gleaning details for the characterization when he has the old Filipino in "Fingers of Cloud" refer to the Kari as a ghoulish female with supernatural powers over anyone who sees her. Steinbeck's "Kari," however, does arrive at the bunkhouse during a thunderstorm; and in the opening scene she wanders away from home to climb a mountain, hoping to touch the clouds. Throughout the story, Steinbeck notes Gertie's attraction to clouds: the story ends as it began, with her wandering away from the "home" Pedro has made for her on a quest to touch the clouds at the top of the mountain.

Though Gertie's character is whimsical and underdeveloped, Steinbeck obviously intended to associate her with the mythic deity of thunder. She even commands respect from Pedro and the other men for a while, as if they believe she possesses supernatural powers; but Gertie has little patience with the men when they begin to show their resentment of her. Likewise, Curley's wife quickly becomes disillusioned with her limited role as the wife of the ranch owner's son, and she dreams of running away to Hollywood, a fantasy almost as far-fetched as the belief that one can touch the clouds. Of course,

42

Steinbeck is not as obvious in his handling of mythic associations in *Of Mice and Men* as he is in "Fingers of Cloud." For example, no one in the novella refers to Curley's wife as Eve, yet she is immediately identified by George as the one person who could ruin his chances for paradise.

As for the real-life counterpart of Curley's wife, Steinbeck was never as forthcoming about her identity as he was about Lennie's. We may assume that her character is a composite. He did, however, explain in a letter to Claire Luce, the actress who played the part on Broadway, that Curley's wife "is a nice, kind girl and not a floozy. No man has ever considered her as anything except a girl to try to make. She has never talked to a man except in the sexual fencing conversation. She is not highly sexed particularly but knows instinctively that if she is to be noticed at all, it will be because some one [*sic*] finds her sexually desirable" (*LL*, 154–55).

Further remarks in the letter deal more specifically with the playscript character than with Curley's wife in the novella, and will be closely examined in the discussion of the play version in chapter 6 of this study. My immediate focus is on Steinbeck's portrayal of this character as someone whose life is severely limited, a sympathetic character. Nonetheless, because the mythic discourse on *Of Mice and Men* dictates the exile from the Garden of Eden (symbolized by the land dream), Candy's assessment of Curley's wife as a "tart" (*OMM*, 28)—and George's ready acceptance of this idea—sustains the Eden myth on one level.

A point that is often overlooked by readers who criticize the misogynistic characterization of Curley's wife is that Steinbeck counters George's stereotypical condemnation of her by undermining the entire scenario of the Garden of Eden story. Before we even know of Curley's wife, for instance, Steinbeck intimates that the paradise of the land dream is doomed. Critics generally agree that the grove in the opening scene where George and Lennie spend the night—the same grove in which George shoots Lennie at the end of the story—symbolizes the dream of owning the farm and living "off the fatta the lan'" (*OMM*, 14). Before the central characters enter the story, Steinbeck sets the scene with a vivid description of the "narrow pool":

[O]n the valley side the water is lined with trees—willows fresh and green with every spring, carrying in their lower leaf junctures the debris of the winter's flooding; and sycamores with mottled, white, recumbent limbs and branches that arch over the pool. On the sandy bank under the trees the leaves lie deep and so crisp that a lizard makes a great skittering if he runs among them. Rabbits come out of the brush to sit on the sand in the evening, and the damp flats are covered with the night tracks of 'coons, and with the spread pads of dogs from the ranches, and with the split-wedge tracks of deer that come to drink in the dark. (*OMM*, 1)

But when Lennie gulps the water from the pool in the grove, George warns him that it might make him sick: "I ain't sure it's good water. Looks kinda scummy" (*OMM*, 3). George's comment reveals that symbolically, at least, paradise may already be spoiled.

Other details of the story also underscore the illusive nature of Eden in *Of Mice and Men*. When George talks about the actual farm that he intends to buy for himself and Lennie, he explains to Candy that he can get the place for the low price of $600 because "[t]he ol' people that owns it is flat bust" (*OMM*, 59). Apparently, the present owners of the farm are not able to live off the fat of the land, a detail that both George and Candy conveniently overlook. Yet Steinbeck, by deliberately bringing this fact to the attention of the reader, creates a tension between George's mythic discourse of the dream life toward which he is striving and the voice of reality, which says that even if he acquires the piece of land he has in mind, his dream of Eden may not be guaranteed. Still, the identification of a real farm at a reasonable price, a price that George believes he will be able to meet, with Candy's help, by the end of the month, sets up a countermovement to the pattern of inevitable failure that is carefully constructed in the first two parts of the story. Lisca notes that this interruption of the pattern of inevitability in the novella creates "the necessary ingredient of free will. The story achieves power through a delicate balance of the protagonists' free will and the force of circumstance" (Lisca 1981, 138).

Moreover, it is the force of circumstance, which we have already seen was very real to many Americans during the 1930s, that gives *Of Mice and Men* both its realistic edge and its accessibility to myth. In

Layers of Complexities: Reality, Symbol, and Myth

The Legacy of Conquest, an analysis of development in the American West after the alleged closing of the frontier in 1890, Patricia Limerick deals with the unavoidable Garden of Eden analogy in the following manner: "When Adam lived in Eden, he lived off the bounty of nature. After he sinned, his conditions of employment took a turn for the worse: he had to earn his bread by the sweat of his brow. If the fall from Eden had followed the patterns of Western American history, Adam would have carried a further burden: he would have sold the crops he produced at an unpredictable, often disappointing price—or he would have worked for wages."[6] As Limerick points out in example after example, most American pioneers did not venture to the western frontier to become wage earners. They came with the intention of staking claims in gold and silver mines, acquiring numerous acres of valuable farming or grazing land, or mastering vast tracts of wilderness and selling the bounty to others; at the very least, these adventurers expected to become self-sufficient property owners, living off the fat of the land.

Though some did "strike it rich" in the West, so to speak, many more lost either their lives or their life savings when confronted with hostile weather conditions, dangerous terrain, and/or native populations unwilling to relinquish their ancestral home to newcomers. Many families and individuals whose enterprises succeeded initially were reduced to poverty during the Great Depression. For those people who had lost everything or who had gained little to begin with, all that could be done was to hire on as wage earners under the lucky entrepreneurs who had won the race for riches on the great frontier and had managed to survive the Depression.

These wage earners, Limerick's fallen Adams, are the prototypes for the central characters in *Of Mice and Men.* The responsibilities of brotherhood and the longing for a return to Eden are major themes in the story, of course. But to fully appreciate Steinbeck's craft, we must understand that this story about two migrant farmworkers with a dream is not simply a realistic novel with mythical biblical overtones. It is also a western American fable in which Steinbeck exposes the pioneering impulse to view people and places as commodities subject to the idiosyncrasies of the marketplace, an impulse that often disguises

45

itself as an idyllic quest for the American dream. The disguise in this case is the surface story in *Of Mice and Men,* which might be read as a sentimental interlude in the lives of two hard-working, down-and-out barley buckers, George Milton and Lennie Small—guys who just want to buy a little place of their own and become self-sufficient. The potential for sentimentality ripens when these two form a coalition with old Candy, the injured farmhand whose days of employment are numbered. Surely George and Lennie will let Candy come and live with them, do some cooking and cleaning, have a little garden of his own. Things seem to be working out fine until that evil entity—Woman, in the person of Curley's wife—enters the picture and makes the passage to paradise impossible.

Though at times it seems that George doubts the possibility of ever owning a farm, his insistence that Lennie believe in the dream results not only from his need to control Lennie's actions but from a sincere commitment to Lennie. Both Louis Owens and William Goldhurst have discussed *Of Mice and Men* in light of the Cain and Abel story. Owens asserts that loneliness is the central theme of the novella and that the story is not as pessimistic as some critics have insisted. If we accept the non-teleological premise of the story, we understand that human beings are flawed and that their hopes of regaining Eden are illusory. Owens believes that the characters' commitment to the dream and to each other, however, is not flawed. He explains: "The dream of George and Lennie represents a desire to defy the curse of Cain and fallen man—to break the pattern of wandering and loneliness imposed on the outcasts and to return to the perfect garden. George and Lennie achieve all of this dream that is possible in the real world: they are their brother's keeper" (Owens 1985, 102). Similarly, Goldhurst offers an allegorical reading of *Of Mice and Men* as Steinbeck's parable of the curse of Cain, delineating the ways in which the question "Am I my brother's keeper?" permeates the story as other characters are affected by the commitment between George and Lennie (Goldhurst, 48–59). Curley is suspicious of it, Slim admires it, and Candy and Crooks briefly participate in the brotherhood by looking after Lennie when George is not around. Although all of the plans for buying the farm are shattered when Lennie dies, Steinbeck still leaves the reader with an image of two men together as George and Slim walk away from the grove by the river where the story had begun.

On another level, however, even while George accepts responsibility for Lennie, he realizes that he must face the harsh realities of keeping such a brother. He takes stock of the situation and makes calculating decisions about his course of action. Lennie, as a natural resource, represents a wealth of physical labor, strength that George tries to harness and turn into earning power for the good of both men. Realizing that few people will make exceptions for Lennie's handicap, George plans to sell himself and his sidekick to the ranch boss as a package deal. On their way to the ranch, George tells Lennie, "We're gonna go in an' see the boss. Now, look—I'll give him the work tickets, but you ain't gonna say a word. You jus' stand there and don't say nothing. If he finds out what a crazy bastard you are, we won't get no job, but if he sees ya work before he hears ya talk, we're set" (*OMM*, 6).

George does not expect the rancher to view his situation humanely—only economically. Unfortunately, Lennie's strength cannot be separated from his essential nature of unpredictable, uncontrollable violence, a power that George only fools himself into thinking he controls. As handler of two men's wages, though, George believes he will be able to get a stake together, buy a small farm, and finally remove Lennie from the working world that he endangers and is endangered by. Such a move will also allow George to escape from the authoritarianism of the workplace that he seems to resent bitterly.

When the boss at the ranch realizes that Lennie is mentally deficient, he questions George: "Say—what you sellin' . . . what stake you got in this guy? You takin' his pay away from him?" (*OMM*, 22). George insists, of course, that he's not selling Lennie out; nevertheless, the confrontation highlights the ranch owner's view of the worker as something less than human, an object subject to the laws of bargaining. Because of the economic factors involved, George and Lennie's story takes on harsh edges—goes beyond a moralistic retelling of Cain and Abel or paradise lost. Lennie becomes the commodity that George must manage, invest in, if you will, in order to save him. George's ownership of Lennie's work power is evidenced, for example, by his

appropriation of Lennie's work ticket. To accuse George of exploitation would be too harsh, but circumstances indicate that without
Lennie's wages added to his own, George wouldn't have a chance of
buying that little farm.

These same economic factors undercut the sentimentality of the
partnership with Candy. George doesn't decide to let Candy in on the
land deal because he has compassion for the old man. Steinbeck obviously solicits sympathy for Candy by drawing out the scene in which
Carlson persuades him to "trade in" his old dog for a new one. Even
here, Steinbeck develops the plot by employing the language of the
"hard sell." Carlson convinces Candy that his dog is of no use to anyone and a misery to himself and others. As effectively as an experienced salesman, Carlson "sells" Candy on the idea of killing the old
dog and selecting a replacement from the litter of puppies in the barn.
George witnesses the scene and no doubt realizes that Candy has been
pressured into doing something that he may regret. Nevertheless, even
after Candy's speech about losing his hand, collecting the compensa-
tion, and putting away extra cash because he anticipates being fired,
George hesitates to make him a partner. But when Candy says, "I'd
make a will an' leave my share to you guys in case I kick off, cause I
ain't got no relatives nor nothing" (*OMM*, 59), suddenly the matter is
settled: George decides to write to the people who own the farm,
make an offer, and send $100 of Candy's money to bind the deal.

Candy thus not only buys his way into the brotherhood, he
promises to will his share of it to George. Steinbeck underscores the
importance of Candy's monetary contribution to the cause by juxta-
posing Candy's acceptance into the brotherhood with Crooks's rejection from it by George. Crooks, who has no cash but can only offer his
labor, is never a serious partner in the land dream. Though he joins in
the discussion with Lennie and Candy about growing a garden and
raising rabbits, as soon as George enters the scene and scolds Candy
and Lennie for making their plans public, Crooks withdraws from the
conversation.

On the other hand, Curley's wife, who also wishes to escape the
ranch, is unable to buy her way into George's brotherhood.
Immediately George "sizes her up" in monetary terms: "Bet she'd clear

out for twenty bucks," he says to Candy after the woman has made her first appearance at the bunkhouse on the pretense of looking for Curley (*OMM*, 32). George underestimates her loneliness and disillusionment, however. Eventually we learn that she will "clear out" for even less than "twenty bucks": she plans to leave the ranch for the mere *promise* of a life in Hollywood where she'll become the girl on the silver screen, wear nice clothes, have many admirers, and live happily ever after. It is not surprising that Steinbeck reserves the emptiest and most commercial of American dreams for Curley's wife. Her desire to be part of an industry that glamorizes the transformation of real people into commodities for commercial exchange emphasizes the very parsimony of choices available to women in the 1930s, even if they had the independent will to reject the traditional role of homemaker.

That Curley's wife views herself as a commodity is evident from details of her make-up and "costume": "She had full, rouged lips and wide-spaced eyes, heavily made up. Her fingernails were red. Her hair hung in little rolled clusters, like sausages. She wore a cotton house dress and red mules, on the insteps of which were little bouquets of red ostrich feathers" (*OMM*, 31). She has cultivated the look of a Hollywood actress or a magazine model, and even her body movements appear to be studied gestures from movies or photographs. When she talks to Lennie and George, "She put her hands behind her back and leaned against the door frame so that her body was thrown forward" (*OMM*, 31). As Lennie's eyes moved down over her body, "she bridled a little" and "looked at her fingernails" (*OMM*, 31). She plays the only role she knows how to play, even though what she really wants is someone to talk to.

Talking to others as a way of defining oneself and exercising power over another person's speech as a way of controlling or limiting that person are concepts that are repeated throughout the story. Several times George warns Lennie not to speak: when they meet the boss, for instance, and after they meet Curley. George also tells Lennie not to talk to Curley's wife. Crooks, too, after his initial attempt to drive Lennie from his room, finally invites Lennie to sit down on a nail keg and begins talking to him about his childhood. After a moment,

Crooks laughs and makes this observation: "A guy can talk to you an' be sure you won't go blabblin. . . . I seen it over an' over—a guy talkin' to another guy and it don't make no difference if he don't hear or understand. The thing is, they're talkin', or they're settin' still not talkin'. It don't make no difference, no difference. . . . It's just the talking. It's just bein' with another guy. That's all" (*OMM*, 70–71).

Curley's wife expresses this same sentiment when, in her most sincere moment in the novella, she says to Lennie, "I get lonely. . . . You can talk to people, but I can't talk to nobody but Curley. Else he gets mad. How'd you like not to talk to anybody?" (*OMM*, 87). Her only defense against the rejection she faces at every turn is her dream of Hollywood fame, which she shares with Lennie: "Coulda been in the movies, an' had nice clothes—all them nice clothes like they wear. An' I coulda sat in them big hotels, an' had pitchers took of me" (*OMM*, 89). In this same scene, we learn that the girl has gotten her notion of stardom from a traveling show actor whom she met at the Riverside Dance Palace, a guy who told her she was a natural for the movies and who promised to write to her as soon as he got back to Hollywood.

Significantly, the dreams held by both Lennie and Curley's wife are shaped by someone else; their words, gestures, even their thoughts come from mimicking others. Free will, in fact, hardly seems to exist for people like Curley's wife and Lennie. Whether George is exercising free will when he shoots Lennie is a more complex issue because of the ambiguity of his character throughout the book. Because Steinbeck uses animal imagery to describe Lennie on several occasions, Lennie can be seen as a symbol of humankind's animal nature. When he drinks from the pool in the grove, for example, he "dabble[s] his big paw in the water" (*OMM*, 3); when he returns to the river at the end of the story, "Lennie appear[s] out of the brush, and he [comes] as silently as a creeping bear moves" (*OMM*, 100). Lisca has pointed out that the name Leonard means "strong or brave as a lion" while George means "husbandman" (Lisca 1981, 139), a detail that confers free will upon George and denies it to Lennie. It is also possible to gain a clearer understanding of this important issue of free will as it applies to the major actions and characters of the story by examining it through the interpretive lens of psychoanalytic strategies.

One possible reading of the story suggests that the two characters, Lennie and George, are different facets of one personality. Obviously, Lennie often functions on the level of the unconscious. His violent responses to fear illustrate that strong, destructive forces loom just beneath the surface of his consciousness. Even hypothetical threats, such as cats eating the rabbits on the imaginary farm, move Lennie to violent outbursts: "'You jus' let 'em try to get the rabbits,' he tells George. 'I'll break their God damn necks. I'll . . . I'll smash 'em with a stick'" (*OMM,* 58). It is also clear that George tries to exert a conscious control over Lennie. George tells Lennie when to speak and to whom; he makes Lennie promise to return to the grove by the river if there is any trouble on the ranch. But as evidenced by the earlier incident in Weed and the fracas in the bunkhouse during which Lennie crushes Curley's hand, George's control of his partner's powerfully destructive physical strength is actually quite tenuous.

In this interpretive frame, we might say that Lennie acts as an extension of George, a powerful id to George's ego. Mark Spilka develops this kind of Freudian reading of the novel, though he does not use the terms *id* and *ego* to describe the relationship between the two characters.[7] Clearly Lennie, without thinking about what he is doing, seems to be carrying out George's wishes when he severely injures Curley in the bunkhouse fight. George has made no secret of his disgust with Curley, having declared, "I'm scared I'm gonna tangle with that bastard myself" (*OMM,* 37). George also instantly detests Curley's wife and honors her with such invectives as "bitch," "poison," and "jail bait" (*OMM,* 32). Even though Lennie responds to the girl sensually and thinks she is "purty," that stroking her hair is "nice" (OMM 32, 91), he eventually becomes the instrument of her destruction.

In an early response to *Of Mice and Men,* Stanley Edgar Hyman argued that readers had drawn erroneous conclusions about the meaning of the story because they failed to recognize "that the book functions on two marked levels, the symbolic and the real, and that despite their vastly different directions and meanings, it has proved hard for

[handwritten margin note: psychoanalytical thinks about.]

[handwritten margin note: Lennie carrying out George's actions that George thinks about.]

most readers to keep them separate" (Tedlock and Wicker, 159). Hyman sees the symbolic message as a purely social one: George, a radical leader, attempts to lead Lennie, a symbol of the masses, to a utopia. Lennie, because he is too strong and too untrustworthy, fails George, and thus the utopia fails. On the realistic level, Hyman argues, George is simply a worker who is trying to get out of his class and move into the owning class. Hyman writes: "This foolhardy ambition collapses, the vessel of George's discontent (Lennie), is killed off, and at the end Steinbeck hints at the formation of new alliance between George and the adjusted worker functioning successfully within his class, Slim" (Tedlock and Wicker, 159).

Both Spilka's and Hyman's analyses of characters and events give reasonable accounts of the partnership between the two central characters; they even suggest that George needs Lennie as much as Lennie needs George. They do not, however, satisfactorily explain why George so vehemently despises Curley's wife or why he kills his partner at the end of the novel. To come to terms with these issues, we must deal with the antagonistic forces within George's psyche, forces that may be interpreted as Jungian archetypes. We know from Carol Henning, Steinbeck's first wife, that Steinbeck's friendship with the Jungian philosopher Joseph Campbell in the early 1930s had a discernible effect on the writer's intellectual development. The two men met frequently at Ed Ricketts's laboratory in Monterey where they discussed ideas and books (Benson, 223–25). Recognizing Steinbeck's familiarity with Jung's work, critics have noted the psychoanalytic influences in the novels *To A God Unknown* and *In Dubious Battle* and in several of the stories in *The Long Valley*. Likewise, Jung's ideas about the ego and the unconscious self are useful in interpreting *Of Mice and Men*. In Jungian terms, Lennie appears to be George's "shadow self" and Curley's wife is his "anima," archetypes that invade the unconscious.[8]

Jung describes both the shadow and the anima, or animus, as projections that "change the world into the replica of one's unknown face" (Jung, 147). The shadow is always of the same gender as the subject and may even be recognized as the subject's evil nature. Jung explains that the shadow self is a projection of the ego's dark characteristics, inferiorities of an emotional, obsessive, or possessive quality. Jung writes: "On this lower level with its uncontrolled or scarcely controlled emotions one behaves more or less like a primitive, who is not only the passive victim of his affects but also singularly incapable of moral judgment" (Jung, 148). Lennie can be seen as a primitive who responds instinctively to various stimuli and is incapable of moral judgment, yet his destructive path is not necessarily random. Lennie manages to harm the people toward whom George harbors animosity. At times George even expresses an extreme dislike of Lennie. He complains that because of Lennie he can't keep a job, or "[g]et a gallon of whiskey, or set in a pool room and play cards or shoot pool" (*OMM,* 11). Ultimately, it is Lennie who brings about the circumstances that allow George to free himself of the illusive land dream and the responsibility of taking care of his mentally deficient partner.

Looking closely at the text, we see that in the opening scene Steinbeck subliminally defines Lennie as George's shadow after first drawing our attention to the river, a symbol of the Jungian collective unconscious. Then, as Lennie follows George into the sycamore grove by the river, Steinbeck underscores the fact that they are dressed exactly alike: in shadow fashion, they walk single file down the path, "and even in the open one stayed behind the other. . . . The first man stopped short in the clearing, and the follower nearly ran over him" (*OMM,* 2–3). After both of them have had a drink of water from the pool, George "replaced his hat, pushed himself back from the river, drew up his knees and embraced them. Lennie, who had been watching, imitated George exactly. He pushed himself back, drew up his knees, embraced them, looked over to George to see whether he had it just right. He pulled his hat down a little more over his eyes, the way George's hat was" (*OMM,* 3–4). The shadow motif is unmistakable in this scene that serves as our introduction to the main characters.

That Lennie has survived as long as he has is proof of George's commitment to his care. Still, the motives underlying that commitment are never clearly delineated. Steinbeck deliberately avoids explaining exactly how Lennie and George became sidekicks. We know that Lennie's Aunt Clara asked George to look after Lennie when she died. George's relationship with Aunt Clara, though, is a mystery; and we haven't a clue as to how long ago she died. We know from George's complaints about never being able to keep a job that the incident in Weed is just one of many unfortunate adventures with Lennie. In fact, Steinbeck tells us very little about their past except that George and Lennie played together as children, and as they grew older George came to realize that Lennie was dumb and could be easily manipulated. George tells Slim, "Used to play jokes on 'im cause he was too dumb to take care of 'imself. But he was too dumb even to know he had a joke played on him. I had fun. Made me seem God damn smart alongside of him. Why he'd do any damn thing I tol' him" (*OMM*, 40).

Then, in "the tone of confession," George relates in more detail the incident at the Sacramento River that put an end to his childhood pranks involving Lennie. In this episode, George is showing off in front of "a bunch of guys," and he tells Lennie to jump in the river, even though Lennie could not swim. "He damn near drowned before we could get him," George tells Slim. "An' he was so damn nice to me for pullin' him out. Clean forgot I told him to jump in. Well, I ain't done nothing like that no more" (*OMM*, 40). The details of this event, while adding to the realistic texture of the story and to character development, also reinforce the Jungian relationship between the conscious self (George) and the unconscious self (Lennie). It is more than coincidence that George's realization of his own responsibility for Lennie's actions occurs in a river, the symbol of Jung's collective unconsciousness.

Nonetheless, it is unclear whether or not George completely grasps the potential danger of Lennie's mindless strength: several times George insists that Lennie "ain't mean," but he also warns that Curley is "gonna get hurt if he messes around with Lennie" because Lennie "don't know no rules" (*OMM*, 27, 28). But George, who presumably does know the rules, doesn't always choose to follow them. He decides, for example, to camp at the river instead of reporting to the ranch in the evening. By arriving at the ranch in the morning instead of the night before, George and Lennie miss half a day of work and incur the ranch owner's anger before he even meets them. This one incident could be an indicator that George's failure to keep a job in the past cannot all be blamed on Lennie. After the tense interview with their new boss, however, George immediately blames Lennie for making the ranch owner suspicious of them.

All of these minor details are indicative of George's violently aggressive nature. Both fearing and repressing the primitive impulses in himself, he projects them onto Lennie. The dream farm represents a haven in which George's aggression (represented by Lennie) can be repressed. George devises the plan to escape from the real world of migrant life—bunkhouses, rough men, whiskey, and whorehouses— because he is disturbed by the qualities in himself that such a life brings to the surface. Unconsciously, he projects undesirable characteristics onto his shadow self, then feels the need to control that self by isolating it in the safe haven of the Edenic dream farm. Meanwhile, George inadvertently directs Lennie toward disaster by staying at the ranch even after the trouble with Curley and by making Lennie fearful of Curley's wife. Though George may realize that Lennie will eventually do something terrible for which he will have to be incarcerated or destroyed, he does not take him away from the ranch because of an unconscious desire to rid himself of his shadow.

A Jungian interpretation of *Of Mice and Men* highlights the conflict of personalities and priorities in the story. It also points to a more thorough understanding of the characterization of Curley's wife than has previously been offered. Just as Lennie may be seen as George's shadow self, Curley's wife has characteristics of the Jungian anima. The contrasexual figure—the animus of woman, and the anima of a man—represents the face of "absolute evil" and is usually not recognized by the subject as part of his or her own psyche (Jung, 148). One face of a man's anima is the seductress, a projection that embodies the negative, unconscious, and unrealized aspects of the psyche to which a man responds with fear. At the same time that the anima arouses libidinal drives within the psyche, a patriarchal consciousness strives to repress the feminine force.[9] For example, the first time that George and Lennie see Curley's wife, Lennie's comment, "Gosh, she was purty" (*OMM*, 32), triggers a violent reaction from George, who grabs his partner by the ear and shakes him:

OF MICE AND MEN

"Listen to me, you crazy bastard," he said fiercely, "don't you
even take a look at that bitch. I don't care what she says and what
she does. I seen 'em poison before, but I never seen no piece of
jail bait worse than her. You leave her be."
    Lennie tried to disengage his ear. "I never done nothing,
George."
    "No, you never. But when she was standin' in the doorway
showin' her legs, you wasn't lookin' the other way, neither."
(OMM, 32)

Though Lennie's comment seems innocent and naïve enough,
George's statements are vicious. He, too, "wasn't lookin' the other
way" when the woman was standing in the doorway; he, too, notices
her appearance and gestures, and his response to her is much more
intense than Lennie's.
    Curley's wife represents a mysterious and autonomous force that
stimulates George's sexual consciousness, challenges his manhood,
inspires self-doubt, and taunts him for his meanness. Throughout the
story, George gives conscious expression to these feelings. For
instance, he admits it is mean of him to lose his temper over Lennie's
wanting ketchup with his beans (OMM, 12); and he tells Slim about
the tricks he played on Lennie when they were youngsters (OMM, 40).
Also, George is reluctant to express himself sexually: when Whit tries
to interest him in visiting Susy's place on Saturday night, he insists that
if he does go to the whorehouse, it will only be to buy whiskey. The
overt sexuality of Curley's wife is an inversion of George's puritanical
nature, and as George's anima she sparks an intensely negative reaction from him. She also serves as a conscious reminder of his longing
to "live so easy and maybe have a girl" (OMM, 7), the dream that he
represses because of his association with Lennie.
    Given the grim socioeconomic circumstances of the laborers and
of Curley's wife, it is reasonable to assume that they dream of escaping
reality. Several times in the novel George expresses the desire to
change his life. Sometimes he imagines himself free of the responsibility of looking after Lennie: he could keep a job and not always have to
be on the move; maybe he could have a girl, or he could go into town
with the guys whenever he wanted to; he could shoot pool, drink

whiskey, etc. At other times he talks about buying the little farm where he could have a garden and Lennie could tend rabbits. These dreams have several elements in common: each represents a change from the status quo and each holds forth some form of freedom for George. Notwithstanding, the two scenarios are mutually exclusive.

In a sense, George's dreams compete throughout the text for actualization and verbalization; and though they are voiced by the same character each time, they are spoken in different "voices." The narrative expletive attached to George's speech about life without Lennie is, "George exploded" (*OMM,* 11). His description of living "so easy" comes out in anger; the words spew forth unrehearsed. In contrast, when George tells Lennie about the farm, his voice "became deeper. He repeated his words rhythmically as though he had said them many times before" (*OMM,* 13). The signal is clear: we are not experiencing George's "voice" as we had been in the present-tense situation of the story, and the words of his speech may not even be his own. The dream-farm litany may simply reflect George's lip service to the promise that he made to Lennie's Aunt Clara, a plan reflecting the illusion of the American dream and a belief in the mythic innocence of a prelapsarian Eden. This close examination of the narrative syntax in the passages related to the competing dreams reveals that Steinbeck consciously created dialogic tension in the text.

To explain the dialogic tension, or double-voicedness, in *Of Mice and Men,* I am borrowing from Mikhail Bakhtin's theory of discourse as dialogue between a speaker and a listener about a hero or subject.[10] In verbal and written utterances, the subject becomes an active agent, interacting with the speaker "to shape language and determine form," and the subject (or hero) often becomes the dominant influence.[11] Dialogic tension exists in all discourse because words, the elements of the dialogue, are loaded with various social nuances that influence one another and perhaps even change as a result of the association. According to Bakhtin, "Each word tastes of the context and contexts in which it has lived its socially charged life; all words and forms are populated by intentions. Contextual overtones . . . are inevitable in the word" (Bakhtin, 293).

Several times in the story George is questioned about his relationship with Lennie; his responses to the questions vary greatly depending on the context of the inquiry and on his relationship with the questioner. When the ranch boss asks George, "Say—what you sellin'?" George responds defensively and lies about Lennie's being his cousin (*OMM*, 22–23). But when Slim observes, "Funny how you an' him string along together," George views the comment as an "invitation to confidence" and tells Slim the truth about his relationship with Lennie (*OMM*, 39). In both of these exchanges, the subject of discussion is George's relationship with Lennie. George is the speaker in both cases, but because the listeners differ, the subject changes shape or form and appears to control the speaker. Like the hero in a piece of fiction, the subject dominates the situation and ultimately determines the speech act.

Steinbeck also manipulates the levels of dialogic tension in the story by having various characters reveal their inner thoughts to Lennie, an uncomprehending listener: George does this, as do Crooks and Curley's wife. In each instance, the characters tell Lennie about their dreams; also, in each instance, the contexts of the speeches to Lennie are more like dialogues between the speaker and the subject than dialogues between two comprehending speakers. Yet having Lennie to talk to gives credence to the utterances. Like George, who is a drifter and thus an outsider wherever he goes, both Curley's wife and Crooks are obviously starved for companionship and acceptance as both are systematically ostracized from the ranch community—Crooks because of race and Curley's wife because of gender.

Part 4, which takes place in the stable buck's room, highlights the dialectical nature of Crooks's discourse. When Lennie first approaches Crooks, the black man warns, "You got no right to come in my room" (*OMM*, 68). Crooks is very territorial about the limited space that has been allotted to him on the ranch. He complains to Lennie, "I don't know what you're doin' in the barn anyway. . . . You ain't no skinner. They's no call for a bucker to come into the barn at all" (*OMM*, 68). Finally, Crooks gruffly invites Lennie to "Come on in and set a while" (*OMM*, 69); as soon as Lennie begins talking about living on a farm and tending to rabbits, Crooks's voice softens and he tells his own story about growing up on the chicken ranch that his father had owned. When Crooks realizes that Lennie really doesn't have the capacity to carry on an interactive conversation, he says, "George can tell you screwy things, and it don't matter. It's just the talking. It's just bein' with another guy. That's all" (*OMM*, 71).

No sooner does Crooks come to this realization than he sets about destroying his own chance to capitalize on Lennie's companionship, the comfort of "just bein' with another guy." Instead of "just talking," Crooks takes advantage of Lennie's feeblemindedness: "His [Crooks's] voice grew soft and persuasive. 'S'pose George don't come back no more. S'pose he took a powder and just ain't coming back. What'll you do then?'" (*OMM*, 71). When Lennie becomes violently defensive of George, Crooks retracts his statements; he moves from chiding Lennie about his dream farm to expressing his longing to participate in the escape.

To reinforce the notion of illusive dreams, Steinbeck also has the girl recount her fantasy of escaping the lonely, restricted life of the ranch. Curley and most of the hired men have gone into town to carouse at the saloons and whorehouses. When Candy, Crooks, and Lennie shun Curley's wife's company on Saturday night, she tells them contemptuously, "I could of went with the shows. Not jus'one, neither. An a guy tol' me he could put me in pitchers" (*OMM*, 78). Just "the weak ones" (*OMM*, 77) have been left behind, and Curley's wife seeks the only companionship available to her. The next day she describes her dream again in a conversation with Lennie in the barn just before he accidentally breaks her neck. Here she tells her story "in a passion of communication, as though she hurried before her listener could be taken away" (*OMM*, 88). With this narrative commentary Steinbeck emphasizes that being able to share one's dream with a sympathetic audience—the companionship implied by such an action—is as important as realizing the dream.

Similarly, the contextual overtones of the dream-farm passages as they play out between George and Lennie are twofold: mythical and communal. Sometimes the description of the land dream is delivered as if it were a religious incantation, as when George deepens his voice and speaks rhythmically. At other times the story is related as dialogue or as a chorus of two or more speakers who combine their "speech acts" (Bakhtin's term) to create a composite image. This happens when Lennie interrupts George's recitation about the farm and is coaxed into completing the story himself (*OMM*, 14). Later, in the bunkhouse, after George has agreed to a partnership with Candy, Steinbeck notes that "each mind was popped into the future when this lovely thing would come about" (*OMM*, 60). With their minds on the future, Lennie, George, and Candy discuss their plan, each one adding a specific detail to the description of life on the farm. Lennie, of course, mentions feeding the rabbits; Candy asks if there will be a stove; and George imagines taking a holiday and going to a carnival, a circus, or a ball game. (*OMM*, 60–61).

Significantly, both Lennie's and Candy's comments deal with specific details of farm life, while George's contribution to this idyllic picture focuses on activities that would take him away from the farm. Though his comments are in keeping with the spirit of camaraderie that flows through the conversation, the thematic shift to nonfarm activities is a subtle clue that George's version of the future does not coincide with that of his partners. What George seems to be doing in this speech is reconciling the mythic vision with the more personal vision of how he would live his life if he did not have to look after Lennie. Though George recites the dream-farm myth, it is possible that he is not really committed to it. After all, the primary reason for acquiring the farm is to remove Lennie from the everyday working world in which he cannot seem to stay out of trouble. While Lennie's presence necessitates keeping the dream alive, his uncontrollable strength and outbursts of violence virtually assure that the dream will not come true.

By introducing both of George's dreams in the opening scene of the story, and by emphasizing the differences in the way they are "voiced," Steinbeck highlights the dialectical nature of the narrative, a tension that is maintained throughout the text. From scene to scene, as George appears to be working conscientiously toward achieving the land dream, he is actually moving closer and closer to the competing dream, which is not really a dream at all but a rather mundane description of the bunkhouse life that might be possible for George if he did not have to worry about Lennie. George's immediate attraction to Slim, along with Slim's reciprocal friendship, substantiates a counter-movement in the story, movement away from the dream-farm impulse. Not until Lennie's death is George free to join the community of men represented by Slim. As the only character in the novel who understands that George did not kill Lennie in self-defense, Slim expresses his approval of George's actions. Then he offers to buy George a drink, and together they walk away from the river grove where Lennie has died. It is important to recall that after the first entrance of Curley's wife and George's negative reaction to her, Lennie cries out instinctively, "I don't like this place, George. This ain't no good place. I wanna get outa here" (*OMM*, 32). But in spite of all the danger signs, signals that even Lennie can translate, George decides to stay at the ranch, a decision that leads ultimately to a resolution of the conflict between George's competing dreams.

Through the dialogical structure of the text, Steinbeck maintains narrative tension without articulating moral judgments. George is neither unreasonable nor unrealistic when he imagines himself unencumbered by his promise to Lennie's Aunt Clara. Still, any moral judgment that might influence our interpretation of the final scene must come from an acceptance or rejection of the inevitability of Lennie's death, a decision that in part depends on our interpretation of Slim's character. At times, Steinbeck seems to be depicting Slim as the ideal man: he is an expert on the job, and the other workers defer to his judgment in both personal and professional matters. He even demonstrates his clout with the boss's son by extracting the promise from Curley not to try to get Lennie fired for crushing his (Curley's) hand. Yet in the matter of killing Candy's dog, Slim sides with Carlson, not a very sympathetic character by any standard. In fact, Slim casts the deciding vote when he says, "Carl's right, Candy. That dog ain't no good to himself. I wisht somebody'd shoot me if I got old an' a cripple" (*OMM*, 45). Slim's comment here extends beyond the situation in question and makes an enormous ethical leap by equating the killing of a useless dog with the killing a seemingly useless person, a person who is "old an' a cripple," an accurate description of Candy himself.

No narrative comment attends this bone-chilling pronouncement except "Candy looked helplessly at him, for Slim's opinions were law" (*OMM*, 45). None of the other men show any reaction to Slim's decision, though "Candy looked for help from face to face" (*OMM*, 45). The incident is not mentioned again until Candy tells George that he should have had the courage to shoot the dog himself instead of letting a stranger do it. Though Steinbeck maintains his unblaming narrative stance in relation to this incident, he makes obvious links between Carlson's shooting of the dog and George's shooting of Lennie with Carlson's gun.

Lennie's death, of course, leads to the inevitable resolution of the narrative tension, but Steinbeck offers few syntactical clues to help the reader decide exactly what motivates George to kill Lennie. As George calmly tells his partner about the farm, he hesitates to raise the pistol even after he hears the footsteps of Curley and the other men. Steinbeck prolongs the inevitable resolution of the crisis with this comment: "The voices came close now. George raised the gun and listened to the voices" (*OMM*, 106). Even at the most dramatic moment, Steinbeck resists the temptation to preach to his readers or to sentimentalize George's actions.

George saves himself from prosecution by claiming that Lennie had the gun when he found him and that the shooting was in self-defense. We should not overlook the fact, however, that by taking Carlson's gun from the bunkhouse before he goes in search of Lennie, George inadvertently fuels the temper of the lynch mob because the men assume that Lennie has stolen Carlson's Luger and is armed. Moreover, Steinbeck illustrates the limits of Slim's control over the other men when Slim fails to persuade Curley to stay at the ranch. By the time Slim verbalizes his judgment on the shooting of Lennie—"You hadda, George. I swear you hadda" (*OMM*, 107)—the "prince of the ranch" appears to have abdicated his power. The men follow Curley in a bloodthirsty chase instead of letting Slim handle the capture and arrest.

Steinbeck further undercuts the significance of Slim's pronouncement by giving Carlson the last word: when Slim and George walk away from the grove together, Carlson says, "Now what the hell ya suppose is eatin' them two guys?" (*OMM*, 107). By ending the novella with a question about George and Slim, Steinbeck leaves the reader with questions as well: Did George have to shoot Lennie? Couldn't Slim have controlled the mob and seen that Lennie was taken into custody by the proper officials? Was Lennie's death at George's hand the inevitable outcome of events, or did George have other choices? In spite of Slim's approval, it is obvious that George was acting willfully when he killed Lennie: he did not have to kill his partner; he chose to do so. Though one could argue that George took Carlson's Luger in order to protect himself and Lennie against the advances of the mob, such a speculation seems unlikely.

It is far more reasonable to assume that George planned to shoot Lennie as soon as he discovered that Lennie had killed Curley's wife. By killing Lennie, George consciously decides to give his friend the only protection available to him. With the fatal pistol shot, George rationalizes that he has sent Lennie off to the dream farm forever. By the time George walks away from the grove with Slim, he has let go of the escape dream for himself as well and has embraced the competing dream of living without Lennie and just being one of the guys. Though Steinbeck lets the reader decide which George speaks through the pistol—the one who creates the world of protected innocence or the one who expresses a desire for freedom—he makes one thing very clear: George's pulling the trigger is a reaction to the voices of a cruel reality from which neither he nor Lennie can escape any longer.

6

Stage and Screen

Of Mice and Men opened on the stage at the Music Box Theatre in New York on 23 November 1937, with Wallace Ford as George, Broderick Crawford as Lennie, and Claire Luce as Curley's wife. It was directed by George S. Kaufman, produced by Sam H. Harris, and ran for 207 performances (*LL,* 142). In April 1938, favored by positive audience responses and laudatory critical reviews, *Of Mice and Men* was designated by the New York Drama Critic's Circle, the association of newspaper and magazine play reviewers, as the best American play of the season.

In spite of these obvious signs of success, Steinbeck told a reporter for the *New York Times* that he saw his experiment to write a novel that could be performed as a play as a flop because he had to do extensive rewriting to transform the story from page to stage.[1] Warren French, in a brief essay, "The First Theatrical Production of Steinbeck's *Of Mice and Men,*" speculates that Steinbeck was referring to a production by a San Francisco labor-theater group, the Theatre Union, which ran in the spring and early summer of 1937. This earliest stage production of the story was performed directly from the novella without a playscript, as Steinbeck had originally intended.

Reviewers either ignored or criticized the performance, citing problems with the stage adaptation and the quality of the actors' training in speech.[2] Steinbeck's characterization of the revision process from novella to play as "extensive rewriting" is also rather curious in light of the final version of the playscript, which follows the novella closely, with two exceptions: an expanded role for Curley's wife and the omission of the concluding action and dialogue after George shoots Lennie.

Steinbeck's remarks are likely less an accurate assessment of the revision process than an indication of his desire to put *Of Mice and Men* behind him and get on with his life: namely, a vacation with his wife Carol and a new writing project, "L'Affaire Lettuceberg," the early manuscript of *The Grapes of Wrath*. Thanks to the commercial success of *Of Mice and Men*, the Steinbecks were planning an extended vacation. In February 1937, Steinbeck wrote to Pascal Covici that he and Carol would sail from California to New York about the first of April and then go on to Europe. Steinbeck hoped to have a draft of the stage play for *Of Mice and Men* ready by the time his freighter reached New York (*LL*, 137).

That Steinbeck's mind was already focused on the material for *The Grapes of Wrath,* even as he worked on the playscript for *Of Mice and Men,* is evident not only in his letters to friends but also in one of the minor alterations he made when converting *Of Mice and Men* from novella to play. When Candy first tells George about the ranch boss, George asks, "Boss the owner?" To which Candy replies, "Naw! Superintendent. Big land company."[3] Big land companies, which play such a prominent role in *The Grapes of Wrath,* are never discussed in the book version of *Of Mice and Men,* and this is the only time they are mentioned in the play.

After the stopover in New York, John and Carol went to the Soviet Union and Scandinavia for several months. When they returned to New York, where preparations for the stage production were underway, George Kaufman invited Steinbeck to his home in Pennsylvania to make the final changes in the script. Finally, there was a meeting of Kaufman, Steinbeck, Sam Harris, and Donald Oenslager (set and lighting designer) at Harris's office on the second floor of the Music Box Theatre. Oenslager reports that "There were both general

George takes the dead mouse away from Lennie in the sycamore grove. From the 1937 Broadway production at the Music Box Theatre.

Photo by Peter Stackpole. Courtesy of the Steinbeck Research Center, San Jose State University, San Jose, Calif.

and detailed discussions on the production. At the conclusion of the meeting, John Steinbeck rose and said that he felt all was in good hands and that his presence was no longer necessary; whereupon he departed for California" (*LL,* 141).

Totally engaged in writing *The Grapes of Wrath,* Steinbeck did not return to New York for opening night, though he wrote to his literary agents that it still "was a pretty exciting night even for us, what with Pat [Covici] sending wires after every act" (*LL,* 143). Later, in a letter to Kaufman, he expressed his gratitude for a job well done: "Sometimes in working, the people in my head become much realler than I am. I have had letters. It seems that for two hours you made your play far more real than its audience and only the play existed. I wish I could transport into some mathematical equation, my feeling, so that it might be a communication unmistakable and unchanging" (*LL,* 144–45). Steinbeck's reference to the stage production as "your play" signifies his emotional distance from the project once he had completed it.

Writing a separate playscript for the story, in fact, appears not to have been Steinbeck's idea at all. A number of people in the New York theater scene had expressed interest in the dramatic possibilities of the book. Capitalizing on this interest, Annie Laurie Williams, the play agent for Elizabeth McIntosh and Mavis Otis's office, showed the novel to Beatrice Kaufman, a representative of Samuel Goldwyn Pictures and the wife of George Kaufman, who responded enthusiastically to the project. He wrote Steinbeck that the work "drops almost naturally into play form and no one knows that better than you" (*LL,* 136).

One revision suggested by Kaufman, that Steinbeck "include a *little* more humor . . . both for its lightening effect and the heightening of the subsequent tragedy by comparison" (*LL,* 136), was evidently ignored by the author. Steinbeck did, however, seriously consider another suggestion by Kaufman, who advised that the second act needed "fresh invention": "You have the two natural scenes for it—the bunkhouse and the negro's room, but I think the girl should come into both these scenes, and that the fight between Lennie and Curley, which will climax Act 2, must be over the girl. I think the girl should have a scene with Lennie *before* the scene in which he kills her. The girl, I think, should be drawn more fully; she is the motivating force of the whole thing and should loom larger" (*LL,* 136).

Though Steinbeck did not carry out Kaufman's suggestions to the letter—Curley's wife is not present during the fight between Lennie and Curley, and the fight is not explicitly about her—Curley's wife does exchange words with George through the bunkhouse window just before Curley enters to pick a fight with Lennie. Steinbeck also ignored the suggestion to add a scene between Curley's wife and Lennie before the barn scene in act 3. Instead, he expands her role in that scene, giving her an opportunity to tell Lennie about her childhood—dialogue that adds a sympathetic dimension to her character. Furthermore, Steinbeck's resistance to making Curley's wife explicitly the cause for the tension between Curley, Lennie, and George substantiates my earlier analysis of the author's intention to undercut the return-to-Eden motif, even though he drew her character in terms of the archetypal temptress.

Even with these revisions, the character of Curley's wife can hardly be described as well developed. Midway through the play's successful run on Broadway, Annie Laurie Williams reported to Steinbeck that actress Claire Luce had some misgivings about her interpretation of the part. In a 1938 letter Steinbeck wrote to Luce, "perhaps if I should tell you a little about [the character] as I know her, it might clear your feeling about her" (*LL,* 154). This letter, though cordial and apparently sincere, in fact supplies few concrete details about Curley's wife. At times in the character sketch, Steinbeck makes biographical references to an individual person; these specific references, however, are interrupted by an authorial discourse describing a character type. Briefly, the discourse even lapses into moral platitude, at which point Steinbeck apologizes for "preaching" to Luce (*LL,* 154).

Though there is only one speaker in the letter, three voices compete for the reader's attention: an objective voice that relates what the social context dictates about Curley's wife, a personal voice in which Steinbeck talks about the particular woman he had in mind when he created the character, and an emotional speaker who demands sympathy from his listener for the person he is describing. The competing narratives of these three voices demonstrate Steinbeck's difficulty in describing Curley's wife beyond her existence in the playscript. They also echo the dialogic tension, or competing narratives, related to Curley's wife in the original story, signaling the power of context over text that shapes her characterization in both the novella and the play.

With Curley's wife, Steinbeck is trying to describe a person whose role is that of a nonperson. Thus he alternates between broad generalizations that use the language of a social worker and vague assumptions that seem to hint at the life and circumstance of a real person. Steinbeck tells Luce that the girl had been nurtured in "an atmosphere of fighting and suspicion," yet she maintained a "natural trustfulness" that constantly led to disappointment (*LL*, 154). Her rigid moral training had taught her "that she must remain a virgin because that was the only way she could get a husband" (*LL*, 154). Having been "trained by threat," she learned to be hard, especially when she was frightened (*LL*, 154).

Presumably, the actress would already have drawn such general conclusions as these after weeks of delivering such lines as, "Nobody never got to me before I was married. I was straight. I tell you I was good. I was. You know Curley. You know he wouldn't stay with me if he wasn't sure" (*OMM*, play, 350). In fact, Curley's wife reveals more specific details about herself in the script of *Of Mice and Men* than Steinbeck supplies for Luce anywhere in the letter. The lines Curley's wife speaks in the barn just before Lennie kills her reveal specific details of her family background: her father was a sign painter and an alcoholic; violent arguments between her parents were a daily occurrence. The girl describes a childhood episode in which her father tried to run away with her, but the authorities stopped him and "put him away." She ends the speech with "I wish we'd went" (*OMM*, play, 371).

These details not only ground the character in a specific past but also allow the audience to hear her voice when she is not engaged in the sexual repartee that constitutes most of her utterances. This passage helps to explain, as well, why this young woman ever considered a life with someone like Curley to be desirable. That she speaks sincerely only to Lennie, an inattentive and uncomprehending listener, signifies Steinbeck's wish to humanize her character for the audience while maintaining her nonperson status with those characters in the play who are supposedly capable of human understanding.

The character description in the letter continues, but Steinbeck, as if realizing he was not telling Luce anything she could not discern for herself from the lines in the play, shifts in midparagraph to present-tense observations that seem relatively more particular than his opening statements: "She is a nice, kind girl and not a floozy. No man has ever considered her as anything except a girl to try to make. She has never talked to a man except in the sexual fencing conversation. She is not highly sexed particularly but knows instinctively that if she is to be noticed at all, it will be because some one [*sic*] finds her sexually desirable" (*LL,* 154–55).

This segment of the description, though only slightly more specific than the passage previously cited, is certainly more subjective. Here Steinbeck has moved from analyzing the girl's environment to specifying the particularly sexual nature of all her social experiences. By insisting on the verbal distinction between what the girl *is* ("nice" and "kind") and what she *is not* (a "floozy"), however, Steinbeck reveals his uncertainty about his audience's perception of her. This apparent uncertainty arises from the disagreement between the discourse of the evil-woman stereotype that permeates the novella and the playscript and the author's presentation of the character through situation, action, speech, and symbol.

Likewise, even as Steinbeck attempts to clarify Luce's understanding of the character she must portray, his explication is complicated by the same dialogic tension between myth and reality that exists in the fiction (see my discussion of this issue in chapter 5). Finally, abandoning any pretense of specific, concrete description of Curley's wife in his letter, Steinbeck writes: "If you knew her, if you could ever break down the thousand little defenses she had built up, you would find a nice person, an honest person, and you would end up by loving her. But such a thing can never happen" (*LL,* 155). What can and does happen in *Of Mice and Men* is that no one loves Curley's wife. She does not even love herself.

Revisions in the story for the play, however, indicate that Steinbeck was aware of the woman's lack of self-worth in the novel and attempted to add an assertive dimension to her character. When she runs into Lennie in the barn, for instance, she has come there to hide her suitcase. She intends to leave Curley as soon as she can sneak away and hitchhike to Hollywood. Instead of merely voicing her dissatisfaction with life on the ranch, she takes specific action; she plans an escape. Yet even in pursuit of her personal vision, she has no solid notion of herself as a worthwhile person. Her dream is to be in pictures—to become a cinematic image that occupies no space in the real world. She even imagines that the clothes she would wear in the movies would be hers to wear all the time. Thus she will always be just an image, the woman from the silver screen.

Steinbeck's emotional appeal to Luce—"If you knew her . . . you would end up by loving her"—underscores the author's frustration with the task of explaining a character out of context whose major function in her fictional text is to be misunderstood, undiscovered as a human being, unknown even to herself. These few lines also reveal Steinbeck's awareness of privileged authorial information that he is unable to impart to his reader. The "you," of course, in Steinbeck's injunction to the actress is not directed to Luce in particular but to an American society in which vulnerable, unfortunate young women must survive. Steinbeck adds, "I hope you won't think I'm preaching," indicating that he was conscious of, perhaps even embarrassed by, the intense moral tone of his appeal.

The character description in the letter closes with that same peculiar mixture of particularity and universality with which Steinbeck began the sketch: "I've known this girl and I'm just trying to tell you what she is like. She is afraid of everyone in the world. You've known girls like that, haven't you? You can see them in Central Park on a hot night. They travel in groups for protection. They pretend to be wise and hard and voluptuous" (*LL,* 155). *Pretend* is the operative verb here, and it is on this question of pretended worldliness versus innate evil that an assessment of Curley's wife depends.

A brief sampling of critical comments from the past three decades suggests that Steinbeck's readers draw various conclusions about the character. Lisca, in *The Wide World of John Steinbeck,* analyzes recurring motifs of language, action, and symbol in the story and identifies Curley's wife as a "mice symbol . . . who threatens [George and Lennie's] dream by bringing with her the harsh realities of the outside world and by arousing Lennie's interest" (138). This statement follows Lisca's discussion of inevitability in the novel, which leads to the conclusion that Curley's wife is just another soft, furry thing doomed to destruction by Lennie. Her death is just the "something" that was bound to happen to ensure the shattering of George and Lennie's illusion. Lisca's assessment of Curley's wife is relatively neutral: she brings "the harsh realities of the outside world" to bear upon the events of the story, but she does not necessarily represent evil.

On the other hand, both Mark Spilka and Howard Levant offer scathing interpretations of Curley's wife. In his essay "Of George and Lennie and Curley's Wife: Sweet Violence in Steinbeck's Eden," Spilka writes: "Steinbeck projects his own hostilities [toward the woman] through George and Lennie. He has himself given this woman no other name but 'Curley's wife,' as if she had no personal identity for him. He has presented her, in the novel, as vain, provocative, vicious . . . and only incidentally lonely" (Spilka, 64–65). According to Spilka, Steinbeck's revision of the female character's role in the play "creates a new imbalance to correct an old one. His sentimentality is the obverse side of his hostility. . . . Only when sexually quiescent—as in death or childhood—can [Curley's wife] win this author's heart" (66). Similarly, Levant observed that she "is characterless, nameless, constantly discontent, so her death inspires none of the sympathy one might feel for a kind or serene woman" (138).

Sandra Beatty, in her analysis of Steinbeck's treatment of women in his plays, suggests that Curley's wife "serves to reinforce the theme of loneliness, isolation, and the idea of a personal dream which is central to the play. She commands both our sympathy and respect because of her naïve yet genuine pursuit of a life-long dream."[4] Along this same line, Louis Owens reasons that woman is not the evil in the mythical garden of Of Mice and Men: "the real serpent is loneliness and the barriers between men and women that create and reinforce this loneliness" (103). Thus Steinbeck allows Curley's wife to share in the "yearning all men have for warm, living contact" (103).

The author's words, as we have seen, do not offer an authoritative or absolute statement on the woman's character that resolves these conflicting critical views. It is not surprising, then, that Claire Luce, wishing to portray the character in the way the playwright had conceived of her, had misgivings about her interpretation. That Steinbeck sincerely tried to satisfy the actress's request for information is apparent, but it is equally clear that his letter could not have helped Luce much.

By countering his stated conviction that to know this character would be to love her with the forlorn declaration that such a thing could never happen, Steinbeck gives us perhaps the most authoritative statement that he can about Curley's wife. What he reveals in that emotional outburst is that neither the context of the play nor the context of the woman's life allows her full humanity; for this reason, her portrait is incomplete. Nevertheless, even decades after its inception, Steinbeck's little story about something that happened has something to tell its audience, not just of mice and men, but also of *women* who may find themselves in a world where they are unknown and therefore unloved.

Just as Steinbeck's revision of the role of Curley's wife makes her a more sympathetic character in the playscript than in the novella, his decision to end the play with George's shooting of Lennie—even though Slim's exoneration of George is omitted—leaves the audience with a more poignant portrait of George than the book does. Instead of having George lie to the mob about the circumstances of the shooting and then walk away from the scene with a friend to buy him a drink while others raise questions about what is going on, the play ends with the pistol shot. George is alone with Lennie's corpse, a portrait of a shattered dream. Whereas the ending of the book highlights the ambiguities of George's character by drawing attention to his competing dream (just being one of the guys), the end of the play emphasizes George's connection to Lennie, his participation in the land dream, and his isolation.

Critics generally agree that Steinbeck achieves a more dramatic effect by ending the play with the pistol shot and that the author's sympathies are with George. In an analysis of ritualistic murders in

Steinbeck's dramas, John Ditsky offers a clear justification for consid-
ering George a benevolent character to the very end of the play:

> When George kills Lennie, it is with George's acknowledgment
> that not only is Lennie's situation quite hopeless, given Curley's
> penchant for retributive violence, but that Lennie's death (he
> being bearer of the fat-of-the-land liturgical commitment) ends
> the dream for that piece of land they have been dreaming after.
> Thus *Of Mice and Men's* denouement is more than simple exem-
> plary euthanasia: it is a form of suicide for George as well. There
> is, in short, no simple, hard lesson of putting out of its misery of a
> larger and more difficult sort of dog.[5]

An early reviewer, Burton Rascoe, after attending the opening performance of *Of Mice and Men* at the Music Box Theatre in New York,
also viewed George as a completely positive character, a man who
"had imagination, a sense of reality, true compassion, and the dream
of life" (Tedlock and Wicker, 64). Rascoe justifies George's action as
"the morality of expediency that must necessarily arise from Nature's
blundering" (Tedlock and Wicker, 65).

Other reviews that appeared during the first few weeks of the
play's opening run stress the uniqueness of the production and the
unformulaic freshness of Steinbeck's script, but they also reveal that
the New York art world did not know quite how to respond to the
earthy realism of the rural life depicted in the play. One review in particular reflects the aesthetic dilemma that a work like *Of Mice and Men*
poses for a cosmopolitan audience. Grenville Vernon, a reviewer for
the *Commonweal,* called Steinbeck a "new and original talent." In
glowing terms, he goes on: "Mr. Steinbeck is not just another hard-
boiled realist, but a poet sensitive to the plight of the unfortunate and
underprivileged, of those inarticulate men and women, without roots
or basic intelligence, who are one of *the* problems of American civi-
lization."[6] Yet Vernon closes with a sentimental, condescending tone
in which he complains about the rough language of the play.

Stark Young's review for the *New Republic,* though more
insightful than Vernon's, focuses primarily on the adaptation process
from book to playscript and avoids dealing with the play as work of

art in its own right. Young admits that he has trouble describing *Of Mice and Men:*

> I have never seen a play quite like it, have no previous acquaintance with the nature of its suspenses, or with the curious artistic satisfaction that its development affords. But from that last point its quality derives, I am sure of that. That is to say you never quite recognize or believe the characters or the active moments; the speech is not compelling as an actual, sharp recording out of life; the locale is not borne in on you as exactly literal, as inevitable realism, an indisputable entity. But the whole of it seems to come off right in its own kind.[7]

What Young appreciated the most about the production was that the "compact impression of the work as a whole is carried over from book to theatre. . . . There is the same kind of lurid unreality, expressed in terms of violent realism in detail and circumstances" (Young, 170).

But perhaps the most telling evidence of Steinbeck's skill as a dramatist can be found in Rascoe's description of the New York audience on the opening night of the play. Rascoe begins by stating that he is glad Steinbeck did not attend the opening because throughout the first act the audience did not know how to respond to what they were witnessing. They "laughed outrageously" at the "tragic heart-breaking lines of George and Lennie" (Tedlock and Wicker, 59). Rascoe confirms that this same kind of reaction from the audience occurred on subsequent evenings of the production. He goes on to say:

> But the consummate art of Steinbeck conquers every time even the more insensitive elements of a New York theater audience before the first act is over. Compassion for the misfits of life, for those who are handicapped by the imponderables of heredity and environments and for those who are warped physically and emotionally, is so deeply and so understandingly felt and expressed by Steinbeck that, before the curtain comes down on the first act, the light, superficially cynical mood of the less sensitive members of the audience has changed, and pity and wonder has taken possession of them. (Tedlock and Wicker, 60).

Thus Rascoe describes what he calls the "aesthetic miracle" of *Of Mice and Men* (Tedlock and Wicker, 57).

With the success of the play on Broadway, movie agents began plying Steinbeck with attractive offers for rights to a screenplay. "The dogs of Hollywood are loose," he wrote to Elizabeth Otis. "I don't intend to go to Hollywood at any price whatever and this is not a hold out" (*LL*, 148). Ironically, after working for months to achieve artistic purity in a little book that would perhaps demythologize the materialism underlying the American dream, Steinbeck found himself being courted by enterprising filmmakers who thrived on perpetuating illusions. Fortunately for movie lovers, Steinbeck relented in his resolution against Hollywood and agreed to work on a film production with director Lewis Milestone.

Milestone had already established himself as a successful adapter of literary works with his production of *All Quiet on the Western Front*. Having read Steinbeck's book and seen the play, he was eager to make a film version of the story. He had Eugene Solow write a screenplay, which he later took to Steinbeck for approval. Steinbeck not only approved the script but took Milestone to see the ranch that had been the scene of the action that had inspired the novella.[8]

Released in Hollywood on 22 December 1939, the film was not a hit at the box office. To boost ticket sales, United Artists even tried to sell the picture as a sex film, with posters depicting Betty Field (Curley's wife) in seductive poses. When judged on its artistic merits, however, the film was highly successful. A "Movie of the Week" reporter for *Life* magazine described the production as a low-budget gamble taken by director Lewis Milestone and producer Hal Roach that paid off in terms of quality: "For its locale, they rented at $25 a day the Agoura Ranch of William Randolph Hearst. For its characters they chose a cast with little box-office appeal, prepared a script O.K.'d by Steinbeck and shot their film in 42 days. The final cost, under $300,000, makes *Of Mice and Men* the most economical Grade A movie to come out of Hollywood in a decade."[9] The film received a best-picture nomination in the same year (1939) that *Gone With the Wind* swept the Oscars. "Over the years," writes Joseph Millichap in his comprehensive study *Steinbeck and Film*, "*Of Mice and Men* has been recognized as a Hollywood classic, and become a staple of film programs" (15).

Building on the ranch scenes introduced to him by Steinbeck, Milestone capitalized on the panoramic California landscape to establish the important theme of balance between man and nature. Solow's screenplay revises the novella only to the extent needed to translate the story from one medium to another. With the innovative use of a prologue before the credits, Milestone introduces George (Burgess Meredith) and Lennie (Lon Chaney, Jr.) on the run from Weed. George and Lennie immerse themselves in an irrigation ditch just as a cloudburst discourages the posse, which gives up the chase. Night has fallen in the next scene as the two bindle stiffs run to catch up to the open boxcar of a moving train. After they are aboard, George closes the door, and the credits appear on the screen as the train fades into the distance. Millichap points out that in these opening scenes, "the emotional mood of the film (fear, frustration, hatred), characterization (George as the leader, Lennie the follower), style (eye-level shots, careful framing in outdoor scenes), and theme (the relationship of human and animal worlds) are all established" (18).

John Mosher, a film reviewer for the *New Yorker,* claims that "Milestone has improved upon the stage production. . . . The action is swift and telling from the start. It is all the more to the director's credit that this is true since there was easy temptation here to hold the camera for vistas of Western landscape—mountains, ranches, and the like."[10] Taking a cue from Steinbeck's expanded role of Curley's wife in the stage version of the story, Milestone gives the woman a name, Mae, and adds a dinner scene at the farmhouse to illustrate the misery of her life with Curley and his father.[11]

In 1981, Robert Blake produced a made-for-television version of the story in which he stars as George, with Randy Quade as Lennie. This version, too, opens with the chase scene after the episode in Weed, and for the most part patterns scenes after the original screenplay. But instead of George and Lennie hopping a train to escape the mob at the beginning of the movie, they visit Aunt Clara's house, where George tries unsuccessfully to sneak away from Lennie. The interjection of this totally fabricated scene sets the tone for the entire film, which is undoubtedly inferior to the original movie. Not only does the episode indicate the inability of teleplay author E. Nick Alexander to handle exposition, but the very presence of a living Aunt Clara undermines the desperateness of George's situation and the burden of his responsibility for Lennie. For the most part, Blake plays a rather smiley-faced, unburdened George. He and Lennie present themselves to the other workers in the mode of a circus act, with George commanding Lennie to do tricks to prove his strength. Furthermore, the musical score, the romanticized presentation of farm labor, the absurd stereotyping of Curley, his father, and Mae in the dinner scene, the constant wide-eyed expressions of Randy Quade, and the exaggerated handling of the killing of Candy's dog all contribute to a rather trivial, hokey, "Hee-Haw" impression of a classic American tragedy.

A much more artistic, sensitive rendering of the story as a tragedy is accomplished in the 1992 Metro-Goldwyn-Mayer version of *Of Mice and Men,* produced by Russ Smith and Gary Sinise, with a screenplay by Horton Foote, noted for his Oscar-winning screenplay for *To Kill a Mockingbird.* Sinise costars as George, with John Malkovich as Lennie and Sherilynn Flynn as Curley's wife. Foote takes a page from the original screenplay by opening with a prologue before the credits, but goes even further than either of the other films to feature George's isolation and his stern understanding both of the hopelessness of Lennie's condition and the illusiveness of the land dream.

The Sinise production opens with George alone in a dark, moving boxcar; bars of sunlight flash across his sad, shell-shocked face. The credits appear, and then George remembers the frantic departure from Weed: the screaming girl in the red dress, the chase, Lennie and himself hiding in the irrigation ditch, and the final jump onto a moving boxcar. By beginning with a portrait of George at the end of the adventure and presenting the story as a flashback, Sinise directs us to the inevitable tragedy of the tale rather than stressing the excitement of an adventure or the sentimental appeal of the sidekick relationship between George and Lennie. Malcovich plays Lennie as a perfect complement to Sinise's George by skillfully combining menacing strength

Lennie strokes Curley's wife's hair. From the 1937 Broadway production at the Music Box Theatre.

Photo by Peter Stackpole. Courtesy of the Steinbeck Research Center, San Jose State University, San Jose, Calif.

and wildness with the helpless bewilderment of a mentally handicapped hobo.

Foote also expands the role of Curley's wife by giving her an extra scene in the barn in which she flirts with George in an innocent, high-school girl manner, asking him if he's ever had a girlfriend. Curley comes in and makes threatening remarks. Instead of using the farcical dinner scene with Mae, Curley, and Curley's father (invented by Solow and exaggerated in the Blake version) or the scene with Curley's wife in Crooks's room, Foote substitutes a brief encounter between George, Lennie, and the girl outside of the bunkhouse on Saturday night after George has retrieved Lennie from Crooks's room.

Crying and obviously distraught, the young woman tells George and Lennie that Curley got mad at her after supper and broke all of her records; then he went into town with the guys and left her all alone on a Saturday night. She notices the bruises on Lennie's face and asks George and Lennie to tell her how Curley got his hand crushed. Having just been abused by Curley herself, her interest in the person who has caused him pain seems neither as seductive nor as sinister as it does in the original story. Through these revisions of the girl's role in the story, Foote manages to make her less a stereotyped seductress and more an abused, lonely young woman in desperate need of understanding and companionship.

Like the original film version, the 1992 MGM production, though not a big ticket seller, was generally appreciated by film critics. A reviewer for *Esquire* referred to Sinise's performance as "unerring" and praised the compatibility of Malkovich and Sinise, who had played the roles of Lennie and George in a 1980 Chicago theater production.[12] Jay Parini, writing for the *New York Times,* applauded the timelessness of "the emotional landscape of the film that is its heart."

Parini praised not just the film but Steinbeck as a storyteller and social critic: "Steinbeck felt a deep empathy with the hobos and drifters, the field hands and destitute families of the Depression era; their stories still resonate today. Perhaps his novels from the 30s keep selling, and movies and plays continue to be produced from them, because no matter how well off we may feel ourselves, something whispers to us that the Georges and Lennies, though removed by 50 years, are not far away."[13] Parini's assessment focuses sharply on one of Steinbeck's greatest accomplishments: his ability to render the kinship of powerlessness with such force that he created a story that has engaged theater and film audiences as well as readers for more than five decades.

Notes and References

Chapter 1

1. Warren French, *The Social Novel at the End of an Era* (Carbondale: Southern Illinois University Press, 1966), 7; hereafter cited in text as French 1966.

2. Cletus E. Daniel, *Bitter Harvest: A History of California Farmworkers, 1870–1941* (Berkeley: University of California Press, 1982), 62–64; hereafter cited in text.

3. Jackson Benson, *The True Adventures of John Steinbeck, Writer* (1984; New York: Penguin Books, 1990), 326; hereafter cited in text.

4. Louis Owens, *The Grapes of Wrath: Trouble in the Promised Land* (Boston: Twayne Publishers, 1989), 3.

5. Anne Loftis, "A Historical Introduction to *Of Mice and Men*," in *The Short Novels of John Steinbeck*, ed. Jackson Benson (Durham, N.C.: Duke University Press, 1990), 39.

Chapter 2

1. Sylvia Cook, "Steinbeck, the People, and the Party," *Steinbeck Quarterly* 15 (Winter/Spring, 1982): 13; hereafter cited in text.

2. John Steinbeck, *Steinbeck: A Life in Letters,* ed. Elaine Steinbeck and Robert Wallsten (New York: Viking Press, 1975), 108; hereafter cited in text as *LL.*

3. Peter Faulkner, *Modernism* (London: Methuen and Co., 1977), 6.

4. John Timmerman, *John Steinbeck's Fiction: The Aesthetic of the Road Taken* (Norman: University of Oklahoma Press, 1986), 11; hereafter cited in text.

5. Richard Astro, *John Steinbeck and Edward F. Ricketts: The Shaping of a Novelist* (Minneapolis: University of Minnesota Press, 1973), 38–60; hereafter cited in text.

6. Peter Lisca, "Escape and Commitment: Two Poles of the Steinbeck Hero," in *Steinbeck: The Man and His Work,* ed. Richard Astro and Tetsumaro Hayashi (Corvallis: Oregon State University Press, 1971), 82; hereafter cited in text as Lisca 1971.

7. Warren French, *John Steinbeck, Revised Edition* (Boston: Twayne Publishers, 1975), 36; hereafter cited in text as French 1975.

Chapter 3

1. E. W. Tedlock, Jr., and C. V. Wicker, eds. *Steinbeck and His Critics* (Albuquerque: University of New Mexico Press, 1957), 43–49; hereafter cited in text.

2. Harry Thornton Moore, *The Novels of John Steinbeck: A First Critical Study* (1939; Port Washington, N.Y.: Kennikat Press, 1968), 5; hereafter cited in text.

3. Alfred Kazin, *On Native Grounds* (1942; New York: Doubleday Anchor Books, 1956), 304–8; hereafter cited in text.

4. Peter Lisca, "Motif and Pattern in *Of Mice and Men,*" *Modern Fiction Studies* 2 (Winter 1956): 228; hereafter cited in text as Lisca 1956.

5. Peter Lisca, *The Wide World of John Steinbeck* (1958; New York: Gordian Press, 1981), 1; hereafter cited in text as Lisca 1981.

6. The references here are taken from the reprint of Goldhurst's article in *The Short Novels of John Steinbeck,* ed. Benson, 48–49.

7. Howard Levant, *The Novels of John Steinbeck: A Critical Study* (Columbia: University of Missouri Press, 1974), 135, 137.

8. Louis Owens, *John Steinbeck's Re-Vision of America* (Athens: University of Georgia Press, 1985), 8; hereafter cited in text.

Chapter 4

1. "The Murder" first appeared in *O.Henry Prize Stories* in 1934; it was anthologized in *The Long Valley* in 1938.

2. John Steinbeck, *Of Mice and Men/Cannery Row* (New York: Viking Penguin, 1986), 2; hereafter cited in text as *OMM.*

Chapter 5

1. Jackson Benson, "Environment as Meaning: John Steinbeck and the Great Central Valley," *Steinbeck Quarterly* 10, no. 1 (1977): 13.

2. John Steinbeck, *The Pastures of Heaven* (New York: Penguin Books, 1982), 64; hereafter cited in text as *PH.*

3. Melanie Mortlock, "The Eden Myth as Paradox: An Allegorical Reading of *The Pastures of Heaven,*" *Steinbeck Quarterly* 11, no. 1 (1978): 11.

4. "Men, Mice, and Mr. Steinbeck," *New York Times,* 5 December 1937; reprinted in *Conversations with John Steinbeck,* ed. Thomas Fensch (Jackson: University Press of Mississippi, 1988), 9.

5. John Steinbeck, "Fingers of Cloud: A Satire on College Protervity [*sic*]," *Stanford Spectator* 2, no. 5 (February 1924): 161–62; hereafter cited in text as "FC."

6. Patricia Nelson Limerick, *The Legacy of Conquest: The Unbroken Past of the American West* (New York: W. W. Norton and Co., 1987), 97.

7. Mark Spilka, "Of George and Lennie and Curley's Wife: Sweet Violence in Steinbeck's Eden," in *The Short Novels of John Steinbeck,* ed. Benson, 59–70; hereafter cited in text.

8. Carl G. Jung, "Aion: Phenomenology of the Self," in *The Portable Jung,* ed. Joseph Campbell (New York: Penguin Books, 1976), 139–62; hereafter cited in text.

9. Bettina L. Knapp, *Women in Twentieth-Century Literature: A Jungian View* (University Park: Pennsylvania State University Press, 1987), 164–65.

10. Mikhail Bakhtin, *The Dialogic Imagination: Four Essays by M. M. Bakhtin,* trans. Caryl Emerson, ed. Michael Holquist (Austin: University of Texas Press, 1981), 154; hereafter cited in text.

11. Charles I. Schuster, "Mikhail Bakhtin as Rhetorical Theorist," *College English* 47 (October 1985): 595.

Chapter 6

1. *New York Times,* 5 December 1937, sec. 12, p. 714.

2. Warren French, "The First Theatrical Production of Steinbeck's *Of Mice and Men,*" *American Literature* 36 (1965): 525–27.

3. John Steinbeck, *Of Mice and Men,* in *Famous American Plays of the 1930s,* ed. Harold Clurman (New York: Dell, 1974), 314; hereafter cited in text as *OMM,* play.

4. Sandra Beatty, "Steinbeck's Play-Women: A Study of the Female Presence in *Of Mice and Men, Burning Bright, The Moon Is Down,* and *Viva Zapata!*" in *Steinbeck's Women: Essay in Criticism,* ed. Tetsumaro Hayashi, Steinbeck Monograph Series, no. 9 (Muncie, Ind.: Steinbeck Society of America, Ball State University, 1979), 7.

5. John Ditsky, "Ritual Murder in Steinbeck's Dramas," *Steinbeck Quarterly* 11, no. 3–4 (Summer–Fall 1978): 73.

6. Grenville Vernon, *Commonweal,* 10 December 1937, 191; hereafter cited in text.

7. Stark Young, *New Republic,* 15 December 1937, 170; hereafter cited in text.

8. Joseph R. Millichap, *Steinbeck and Film* (New York: Frederick Ungar Publishing Co., 1983), 14; hereafter cited in text.

9. "Movie of the Week: *Of Mice and Men,*" *Life* 8 January 1940, 42–43.

10. John Mosher, "The Current Cinema: Milestone's Mice," *New Yorker,* 17 February 1940.

11. For a scene-by-scene description of the Milestone film, see Millichap, 17–26.

12. Patrick Goldstein, "Gary Sinise Goes to Hollywood," *Esquire,* November 1992, 18.

13. Jay Parini, "Of Bindlestiffs, Bad Times, Mice and Men," *New York Times,* 27 September 1992, sec. H, p. 24.

Selected Bibliography

Primary Works

Novels and Plays

Of Mice and Men is widely available in paperback through Penguin Books, the edition used in this study.

The Acts of King Arthur and His Noble Knights. Edited by Chase Horton. New York: Farrar, Straus and Giroux, 1976.

Burning Bright. New York: Viking Press, 1950.

Burning Bright: A Play in Three Acts. New York: Dramatists' Play Service, 1951.

Cannery Row. New York: Viking Press, 1945.

Cup of Gold: A Life of Henry Morgan, Buccaneer, with Occasional References to History. New York: Robert M. McBride, 1929.

East of Eden. New York: Viking Press, 1952.

The Grapes of Wrath. New York: Viking Press, 1939.

In Dubious Battle. New York: Covici-Friede, 1936.

The Long Valley. New York: Viking Press, 1938.

The Moon Is Down. New York: Viking Press, 1942.

The Moon Is Down: A Play in Two Parts. New York: Dramatists' Play Service, 1942.

Of Mice and Men. New York: Covici-Friede, 1937.
Of Mice and Men: A Play in Three Parts. New York: Covici-Friede, 1937.
The Pastures of Heaven. New York: Brewer, Warren and Putnam, 1932.
The Pearl. New York: Viking Press, 1947.
The Red Pony. New York: Covici-Friede, 1937.
The Short Reign of Pippin IV: A Fabrication. New York: Viking Press, 1957.
Sweet Thursday. New York: Viking Press, 1954.
To a God Unknown. New York: Robert O. Ballou, 1933.
Tortilla Flat. New York: Covici-Friede, 1935.
Viva Zapata! Edited by Robert E. Morsberger. New York: Viking Press, 1975.
The Wayward Bus. New York: Viking Press, 1947.
The Winter of Our Discontent. New York: Viking Press, 1961.

Nonfiction

America and Americans. New York: Viking Press, 1966.
Bombs Away: The Story of a Bomber Team. New York: Viking Press, 1942.
The Forgotten Village. New York: Viking Press, 1941.
Journal of a Novel: The East of Eden Letters. New York: Viking Press, 1969.
John Steinbeck on Writing. Edited by Tetsumaro Hayashi. Steinbeck Essay Series, no. 2. Muncie, Ind.: Steinbeck Research Institute, Ball State University, 1988.
Letters to Elizabeth: A Selection of Letters from John Steinbeck to Elizabeth Otis. Edited by Florian J. Shasky and Susan F. Riggs. San Francisco: Book Club of California, 1978.
The Log from the Sea of Cortez. New York: Viking Press, 1951. The narrative portion of *Sea of Cortez: A Leisurely Journal of Travel and Research,* 1941. With preface "About Ed Ricketts."
Once There Was a War. New York: Viking Press, 1958.
A Russian Journal. New York: Viking Press, 1948.
Steinbeck: A Life in Letters. Edited by Elaine Steinbeck and Robert Wallsten. New York: Viking Press, 1975.
Their Blood Is Strong. San Francisco: Simon J. Lubin Society of California, 1938.
Travels with Charley in Search of America. New York: Viking Press, 1962.
Vanderbilt Clinic. New York: Presbyterian Hospital, 1947.

Secondary Works

Book-Length Critical Studies and Collections

Astro, Richard. *John Steinbeck and Edward F. Ricketts: The Shaping of a Novelist*. Minneapolis: University of Minnesota Press, 1973.

_____, and Tetsumaro Hayashi, eds. *Steinbeck: The Man and His Work*. Corvallis: Oregon State University Press, 1971.

Benson, Jackson J., ed. *The Short Novels of John Steinbeck*. Durham, N.C.: Duke University Press, 1990.

Bloom, Harold, ed. *John Steinbeck: Modern Critical Views*. New York: Chelsea House Publishers, 1987.

Davis, Robert Murray, ed. *Steinbeck: A Collection of Critical Essays*. Englewood Cliffs, N.J.: Prentice-Hall, 1972.

Ditsky, John. *John Steinbeck: Life, Work, and Criticism*. Fredericton, New Brunswick, Canada: York, 1985.

Fensch, Thomas. *Conversations with John Steinbeck*. Literary Conversations Series. Jackson: University Press of Mississippi, 1989.

_____, ed. *Steinbeck and Covici: The Story of a Friendship*. Middlebury, Vt.: Paul S. Ericksson, 1979.

Ferrell, Keith. *John Steinbeck: The Voice of the Land*. New York: M. Evans and Co., 1986.

Fontenrose, Joseph. *John Steinbeck: An Introduction and Interpretation*. New York: Barnes and Noble, 1963.

French, Warren. *John Steinbeck, Revised Edition*. Boston: Twayne Publishers, 1975.

_____. *The Social Novel at the End of an Era*. Carbondale: Southern Illinois University Press, 1966.

Garcia, Reloy. *Steinbeck and D. H. Lawrence: Fictive Voices and Ethical Imperative*. Steinbeck Monograph Series, no. 2, 1972. Muncie, Ind.: Steinbeck Society of America, Ball State University, 1972.

Gladstein, Mimi R. *The Indestructible Woman in the Works of Faulkner, Hemingway, and Steinbeck*. Ann Arbor: UMI Research Press, 1986.

Hayashi, Tetsumaro, ed. *John Steinbeck: A Dictionary of His Fictional Characters*. Metuchen, N.J.: Scarecrow Press, 1976.

_____. *A New Study Guide to Steinbeck's Major Works, with Critical Explications*. Metuchen, N.J.: Scarecrow Press, 1993.

_____. *A Study Guide to Steinbeck: A Handbook to His Major Works*. Metuchen, N.J.: Scarecrow Press, 1974.

Hayashi, Tetsumaro, Yasuo Hashiguchi, and Richard F. Peterson, eds. *John*

Steinbeck East and West. Steinbeck Monograph Series, no. 8. Muncie, Ind.: Steinbeck Society of America, Ball State University, 1978.

Hayashi, Tetsumaro, and Richard F. Peterson, eds. *Steinbeck's Women: Essays in Criticism.* Steinbeck Monograph Series, no. 9. Muncie, Ind.: Steinbeck Society of America, Ball State University, 1979.

Jain, Sunita. *John Steinbeck's Concept of Man: A Critical Study of His Novels.* New Delhi: New Statesman, 1979.

Levant, Howard. *The Novels of John Steinbeck: A Critical Study.* Columbia: University of Missouri Press, 1974.

Lisca, Peter. *John Steinbeck: Nature and Myth.* New York: Crowell, 1978.

_____. *The Wide World of John Steinbeck.* New Brunswick, N.J.: Rutgers University Press, 1958; reprint, New York: Gordian Press, 1981.

McCarthy, Paul. *John Steinbeck.* Modern Literary Monograph Series. New York: Ungar, 1980.

Marks, Lester J. *Thematic Design in the Novels of John Steinbeck.* The Hague: Mouton, 1969.

Martin, Stoddard. *California Writers: Jack London, John Steinbeck, the Tough Guys.* New York: St. Martin's Press, 1983.

Millichap, Joseph R. *Steinbeck and Film.* New York: Frederick Ungar, 1983.

Moore, Harry T. *The Novels of John Steinbeck.* Chicago: Normandie House, 1939.

Owens, Louis. *John Steinbeck's Re-Vision of America.* Athens: University of Georgia Press, 1985.

Pratt, John C. *John Steinbeck.* Grand Rapids, Mich.: Erdmans, 1970.

St. Pierre, Brian. *John Steinbeck: The California Years.* San Francisco: Chronicle Books, 1983.

Tedlock, E. W., and C. V. Wicker. *Steinbeck and His Critics: A Record of Twenty-Five Years.* Albuquerque: University of New Mexico Press, 1957.

Timmerman, John H. *John Steinbeck's Fiction: The Aesthetics of the Road Taken.* Norman: University of Oklahoma Press, 1986.

Watt, F. *Steinbeck.* New York: Grove Press, 1962; reprint, New York: Chips, 1978.

Yano, Shigehary, Tetsumaro Hayashi, Richard F. Peterson, and Yasuo Hashiguchi, eds. *John Steinbeck: From Salinas to the World: Proceedings of the Second International Steinbeck Congress, August 1–8, 1984.* Tokyo, Japan: Gaku Shobo Press, 1986.

Articles and Essays

Beatty, Sandra. "Steinbeck's Play-Women: A Study of the Female Presence in *Of Mice and Men, Burning Bright, The Moon Is Down,* and *Viva*

Selected Bibliography

Zapata!" In *Steinbeck's Women: Essays in Criticism,* edited by Tetsumaro Hayashi and Richard F. Peterson, 7–16. Muncie, Ind.: Steinbeck Society of America, Ball State University, 1979.

Bellman, Samuel I. "Control and Freedom in Steinbeck's *Of Mice and Men.*" *CEA Critic: An Official Journal of the College English Association* 38 (1975): 25–27.

Brown, Daniel R. "The Natural Man in John Steinbeck's Non-teleological Tales." *Ball State University Forum* 7, no. 2 (Spring 1966): 47–52.

Brown, John Mason. "Mr. Steinbeck's *Of Mice and Men.*" In *Two on the Aisle: Ten Years of the American Theatre in Performance,* 183–87. 2d ed. Port Washington, N.Y.: Kennikat Press, 1966.

Brown, Joyce D. C. "Animal Symbolism and Imagery in John Steinbeck's Fiction from 1929 through 1939." *DAI* (Southern Mississippi University) 33 (1972): 1716A.

Cardullo, Robert. "The Function of Candy in *Of Mice and Men.*" *Notes on Contemporary Literature* 12 (1982): 10.

Dacus, Lee. "Lennie as Christian in *Of Mice and Men.*" *Southwestern American Literature* 4 (1974): 87–91.

Davidson, Richard A. "An Overlooked Musical Version of *Of Mice and Men.*" *Steinbeck Quarterly* 16 (1983): 9–16.

Ditsky, John. "Land Nostalgia in the Novels of Faulkner, Cather, and Steinbeck." *DAI* (New York University) 28 (1967): 1072A.

_____. "Ritual Murder in Steinbeck's Dramas." *Steinbeck Quarterly* 11 (1978): 72–76.

Dusenbury, Winifred Loesch. "Homelessness." In *The Theme of Loneliness in Modern American Drama,* 44–51. Gainesville: University of Florida Press, 1960.

Everson, William K. "Thoughts on a Great Adaptation." In *The Modern American Novel and the Movies,* edited by Gerald Peary and Roger Shatzkin, 63–69. New York: Ungar, 1978.

French, Warren. "End of a Dream." In *Steinbeck: A Collection of Critical Essays,* edited by Robert Murray Davis, 63–69. Englewood Cliffs, N.J.: Prentice-Hall, 1972.

_____. "The First Theatrical Production of Steinbeck's *Of Mice and Men.*" *American Literature* 36 (1965): 525–57.

Ganapathy, R. "Steinbeck's *Of Mice and Men:* A Study of Lyricism through Primitivism." *Literary Criterion* 5 (1962): 101–4.

Gladstein, Mimi Reisel. "Female Characters in Steinbeck: Minor Characters of Major Importance?" In *Steinbeck's Women: Essays in Criticism,* edited by Tetsumaro Hayashi and Richard F. Peterson, 17–25. Muncie, Ind.: Steinbeck Society of America, Ball State University, 1979.

Goldhurst, William. "*Of Mice and Men:* John Steinbeck's Parable of the Curse of Cain." *Western American Literature* 6 (1971): 123–35. Reprinted in *The Short Novels of John Steinbeck,* edited by Jackson J. Benson, 48–59. Durham, N.C.: Duke University Press, 1990.

Hadella, Charlotte. "*Of Mice and Men* (1937)." In *A New Study Guide to Steinbeck's Major Works, with Critical Explications,* edited by Tetsumaro Hayashi, 139–63. Metuchen, N.J.: Scarecrow Press, 1993.

Isaacs, E. J. R. "*Of Mice and Men.*" In *Theatre Arts Anthology: A Record and a Prophecy,* edited by Rosamond Gilder et al., 644–46. New York: Theatre Arts Books, 1950.

Jones, Claude E. "Proletarian Writing and John Steinbeck." *Sewanee Review* 48 (October 1940): 445–56.

Levant, Howard. "Three Play-Novelettes." In *The Novels of John Steinbeck: A Critical Study,* 1–9. Columbia: University of Missouri Press, 1974.

Lisca, Peter. "Escape and Commitment: Two Poles of the Steinbeck Hero." In *Steinbeck: The Man and His Work,* edited by Richard Astro and Tetsumaro Hayashi, 75–88. Corvallis: Oregon State University Press, 1971.

_____. "Motif and Pattern in *Of Mice and Men. Modern Fiction Studies* 2 (1956–57): 228–34.

Loftis, Anne. "A Historical Introduction to *Of Mice and Men.*" In *The Short Novels of John Steinbeck,* edited by Jackson J. Benson, 39–47. Durham, N.C.: Duke University Press, 1990.

Morsberger, Robert E. "Play It Again, Lennie and George." *Steinbeck Quarterly* 15 (1982): 123–26.

_____. "Steinbeck's Happy Hookers." *Steinbeck Quarterly* 9 (1976): 101–15. Reprinted in *Steinbeck's Women: Essays in Criticism,* edited by Tetsumaro Hayashi and Richard F. Peterson, 36–48. Muncie, Ind.: Steinbeck Society of America, Ball State University, 1979.

Nossen, Evon. "The Best-Man Theme in the Work of John Steinbeck." *Ball State University Forum* 7, no. 2 (Spring 1966): 52–64.

Pizer, Donald. "John Steinbeck and American Naturalism." *Steinbeck Quarterly* 9 (1976): 12–15.

Roane, Margaret C. "John Steinbeck as a Spokesman for the Mentally Retarded." *Wisconsin Studies in Contemporary Literature* 5 (Summer 1964): 127–32.

Shurgot, Michael W. "A Game of Cards in Steinbeck's *Of Mice and Men.*" *Steinbeck Quarterly* 15 (1982): 38–43.

Spilka, Mark. "Of George and Lennie and Curley's Wife: Sweet Violence in Steinbeck's Eden." *Modern Fiction Studies* 20 (1974). Reprinted in *The Short Novels of John Steinbeck,* edited by Jackson J. Benson, 59–70. Durham, N.C.: Duke University Press, 1990.

Selected Bibliography

Steele, Joan. "A Century of Idiots: *Barnaby Rudge* and *Of Mice and Men*." *Steinbeck Quarterly* 5 (Winter 1972): 8–17.

Biographies

Benson, Jackson. *The True Adventures of John Steinbeck, Writer*. New York: Viking Press, 1984.

Kiernan, Thomas. *The Intricate Music: A Biography of John Steinbeck*. Boston: Little, Brown, 1979.

Valjean, Nelson. *John Steinbeck: The Errant Knight: An Intimate Biography of His California Years*. San Francisco: Chronicle Books, 1975.

Bibliographies

DeMott, Robert. *Steinbeck's Reading: A Catalogue of Books Owned and Borrowed*. New York: Garland, 1984.

Gross, John, and Lee Richard Hayman. *John Steinbeck: A Guide to the Collection of the Salinas Public Library*. Salinas, Calif.: Salinas Public Library, 1979.

Hayashi, Tetsumaro. *A Handbook for Steinbeck Collectors, Librarians, and Scholars*. Steinbeck Monograph Series, no. 11. Muncie, Ind.: Steinbeck Society, Ball State University, 1981.

_____. *A New Steinbeck Bibliography: 1929–1971*. Metuchen, N.J.: Scarecrow Press, 1973.

_____. *A New Steinbeck Bibliography: 1971–1981*. Metuchen, N.J.: Scarecrow Press, 1983.

_____. *A Student's Guide to Steinbeck's Literature: Primary and Secondary Sources*. Steinbeck Bibliography Series, no. 1. Steinbeck Research Institute, Muncie, Ind.: Ball State University, 1989.

Woodress, James. "John Steinbeck." In *American Fiction, 1900–1950: A Guide to Information Sources*, 183–93. Detroit: Gale Research Co., 1974.

Index

Agrarian conflict novels, 4
Agriculture industry, 6–7; labor problems in, 4, 5–6; wages in, 5
Albee, George, 34
Alexander, E. Nick, 78
American dream, 3, 15, 23, 45, 49, 57
Astro, Richard, 13, 14, 21

Back-to-the-farm movement, 3
Bakhtin, Mikhail, 57
Beach, Joseph Warren, 18–19
Beatty, Sandra, 72
Benson, Jackson, 5, 10–11, 12, 40
Blake, Robert, 77, 78, 80
Burgum, Edwin Berry, 19
Burns, Robert, 39

Cain and Abel story, 21–22, 46. *See also* Eden motif
California: agriculture industry in, 4, 6, 7; as American Eden, 34, 39; as setting for film, 77

Campbell, Joseph, 52
Candy (character), 18, 30–31, 41, 46, 48, 60, 61–62
Cannery and Agricultural Workers' Industrial Union, 5
Carlson (character), 30–31, 48, 61, 62
Champney, Freeman, 20
Cheney, Lon, Jr., 77
Collective unconscious, 16; archetypes in, 52; river as symbol of, 53, 54
Communist party, 5, 15–16
Cook, Sylvia, 8, 15–16
Covici, Pascal, 65, 67
Crawford, Broderick, 64
Crooks (character), 18, 31, 48, 49–50, 58–59
Curley's wife (character), 29, 42–43, 48–49, 58, 68–69, 70, 71–73; as anima, 56; and Lennie, 32, 40, 50, 55–56, 59, 68, 69; in playscript, 43, 67–68, 69–70, 73; in screenplays, 77, 80

Daniel, Cletus E.: *Bitter Harvest*, 7
Dialogue, 10, 57, 59–60, 61, 69, 70
Ditsky, John, 74

Eden motif, 34, 37, 39, 40, 43–46, 57, 68; woman in, 40, 46, 68

Faulkner, William, 33
Field, Betty, 76
Flynn, Sherilynn, 78
Foote, Horton, 78, 80
Ford, Wallace, 64
Free will, 50
French, Warren, 15, 23, 64; *John Steinbeck*, 22; *The Social Novel at the End of an Era*, 3

George Milton (character), 34, 35, 38, 39, 52–58, 61–63, 73–74; and Curley's wife, 41, 43, 48–49, 51, 52, 55–56; and land dream, 44, 46, 48, 57, 60, 74; and Lennie, 14–15, 36, 46–48, 50–52, 53–55, 73
Goldhurst, William, 21–22, 46
Great Depression, 3–4, 5, 45
Group man, 6, 8

Harris, Sam H., 64, 65
Hawthorne, Nathaniel, 23
Hemingway, Ernest, 10
Hyman, Stanley Edgar, 51–52

Illegal immigrants, 4

James, Henry, 23
Jung, C. G., 52–53

Kari, 43
Kaufmann, Beatrice, 67
Kaufmann, George S., 12, 64, 65, 67

Kazin, Alfred: *On Native Grounds*, 19
Kennedy, John S., 20

Lennie Small (character), 20, 31–32, 39, 40, 50, 54; and George, 14–15, 36, 46–48, 51–52, 53; killing of, 14, 32, 50, 61, 62, 73, 74; and land dream, 14, 36, 39, 60
Levant, Howard, 72; *The Novels of John Steinbeck*, 22
Limerick, Patricia: *The Legacy of Conquest*, 45
Lisca, Peter, 14–15, 49; *The Wide World of John Steinbeck*, 20–21, 71–72
Loftis, Anne, 7
Luce, Claire, 43, 64, 68, 69, 73

Malkovich, John, 78, 80
Meredith, Burgess, 77
McIntosh, Mavis, 9, 10, 34, 67
Melville, Herman, 23
Metaphor, 34
Migrant farm workers, 4, 5, 9
Milestone, Lewis, 76, 77
Miller, Ted, 10
Millichap, Joseph: *Steinbeck and Film*, 76–77
Moore, Harry Thornton: *The Novels of John Steinbeck*, 19
Mortlock, Melanie, 38
Mosher, John, 77
Music Box Theatre (New York), 64, 65, 74

Naturalistic writing, 22–23
Non-teleological thinking, 8, 12–14, 22, 46

Oenslager, Donald, 65, 67
Otis, Elizabeth, 10, 11, 67, 76

Index

Owens, Louis, 6, 46, 72; *John Steinbeck's Re-Vision of America*, 23, 34

Paisanos, 5
Parini, Jay, 80–81
Play-novella form, 10, 12, 22, 27–32

Quade, Randy, 77, 78

Rascoe, Burton, 18, 23, 74, 75–76
Ricketts, Ed, 12, 13, 14, 52
Roach, Hal, 76

Self and shadow self, 35, 52–55
Sinise, Gary, 78, 80
Slim (character), 29, 30, 39, 52, 61, 62
Smith, Russ, 78
Solow, Eugene, 76, 77, 80
Spilka, Mark, 51, 52, 72
Spreckles Sugar Ranches, 4, 10
Steinbeck, Carol Henning (first wife), 5, 11, 52, 65
Steinbeck, John: artistic aims, 9, 10; birth, 4; on criticism, 17, 24; education, 4; marriages, 11; in Mexico, 5; political views, 4, 6, 15–16; on popularity, 10; prose style, 10

NONFICTION
"Critics—From a Writer's Viewpoint," 17
"Letter on Criticism, A," 17, 24
Log from the Sea of Cortez, The, 13
Sea of Cortez (with Ed Ricketts), 13

NOVELS
Burning Bright, 22
Cannery Row, 22, 23
Cup of Gold, 13
East of Eden, 22

Grapes of Wrath, The, 4, 6, 11, 16, 19, 22, 23, 65; social message in, 15–16, 21
In Dubious Battle, 4, 6, 12, 16, 20, 23, 52; criticism of, 9; sales of, 8
Moon Is Down, The, 22
Of Mice and Men, 4, 6, 8, 12–13, 28–32, 39–63; BOMC selection, 10, 18; characterization in, 7, 14–15, 18, 20, 29–31, 43 (*see also* individual characters); critical response to, 18–24; and dream of owning land, 5, 6, 14, 21, 31, 39, 48, 59–60 (*see also* Lennie Small, and land dream; George Milton, and land dream); as film, 18, 76–80; Freudian reading of, 51; Jungian reading of, 52–55; and non-teleological thinking, 13–14, 46; as play, 18, 43, 64–76; as play-novella, 11, 18, 28–32; public response to, 23, 65; recurring motifs in, 14, 20, 21, 34, 39 (*see also* Eden motif); thematic reading of, 15–16; as television movie, 77–78; writing of, 27
Red Pony, The, 22
To a God Unknown, 13, 52
Tortilla Flat, 5, 23; public response to, 8, 17–18
Wayward Bus, The, 5

SHORT STORIES
"Fingers of Cloud," 5, 40–43
Long Valley, The (collection), 16, 52
"Murder, The," 27
Pastures of Heaven, The (collection), 22, 34–38

SHORT STORIES *(continued)*
"Raid, The," 6
"Vigilante, The," 6

Theatre Union (San Francisco), 12, 64
Timmerman, John H., 10, 12–13;
   John Steinbeck's Fiction, 23, 33

Tortilla Flat, 8
Vernon, Grenville, 74

Whitaker, Francis, 6
Williams, Annie Laurie, 67, 68

Young, Stark, 74–75

The Author

Charlotte Cook Hadella is associate professor of English at Southern Oregon State College. She holds an M.A. in English from Virginia Polytechnic Institute and State University and a Ph.D. in American literature from the University of New Mexico. Her essays on John Steinbeck's work have been widely published in journals and anthologies and her contributions have appeared in *American Literary Scholarship*.